"Over the course of twenty-seven appearances on *The Ellen DeGeneres Show*, I saw Steve Spangler turn science segments into unforgettable shared experiences—moments that sparked joy, curiosity, and connection for millions. *The Engagement Effect* captures that same energy and breaks down the how and why behind it all. This book is Steve at his best."

—Chris Cucci, Producer, *The Ellen DeGeneres Show*

"There's something truly electric about watching fifteen thousand students, teachers, and parents fill Coors Field for our annual STEM Day with Steve Spangler. That kind of excitement and connection doesn't happen by accident—it's the result of intentional strategies that make every individual feel seen, involved, and inspired. In *The Engagement Effect*, Steve reveals the same powerful techniques he's used to make STEM Day one of our most impactful events. This book is an excellent tool on how to captivate an audience and turn engagement into action."

—Greg Feasel, President and Chief Operating Officer, Colorado Rockies Baseball

"For decades, I've had a front-row seat to Steve Spangler's ability to turn everyday television into something unforgettable. He doesn't just demonstrate science—he creates shared moments filled with wonder, laughter, and meaning. *The Engagement Effect* is full of heart, humor, and the kind of insight that turns information into inspiration."

—Kim Christiansen, Anchor, 9NEWS Denver

"The strongest brands don't just sell products—they create experiences that connect, inspire, and build trust. That's what we saw when Excelligence acquired Steve Spangler Science. Steve's work has always gone beyond science, products, and speaking; it's about sparking curiosity and cultivating engagement. *The Engagement Effect* distills that mission into a powerful playbook for leaders and educators who want to elevate every interaction into something meaningful, memorable, and transformative."

—Anupam Martins, Chief Executive Officer, Excelligence Learning Corporation

"At NAFEPA, we focus on translating national education goals into meaningful impact at the state and local levels. Steve Spangler has helped our leaders do just that—bringing his strategies to life with energy, purpose, and clarity. *The Engagement Effect* offers that same spark in written form. It's a powerful resource for anyone looking to turn ideas into real connection and lasting change."

—Bobby J. Burns, Executive Director, National Association of Federal Education Programs (NAFEPA)

"What Steve Spangler offers in *The Engagement Effect* is more than a strategy—it's a mindset. He shows us that true leadership is about creating experiences that make people feel seen, inspired, and ready to grow. This book is a master class in transformational connection."

—Dr. Nido R. Qubein, President, High Point University

"We've trusted Steve Spangler to help us create unforgettable moments for hundreds of thousands of educators at Get Your Teach On—and he always delivers. This book brings his passion, creativity, and practical strategies to the page. If you want to inspire people and leave a lasting impact, this is your playbook."

—Hope & Wade King, Cofounders, Get Your Teach On

"Few people understand the power of engagement like Steve Spangler. I had the opportunity to read *The Engagement Effect* early on, and even then, it was clear—this book has the potential to transform how we lead, teach, and connect. It's a timely, essential guide for anyone who wants to make their message matter."

—Skip Prichard, President and CEO, OCLC; Author of *The Book of Mistakes*

"For more than twenty-five years, Steve Spangler has brought science to life on 9NEWS through over 1,800 unforgettable segments—each one designed to spark wonder, ignite curiosity, and inspire joy. In *The Engagement Effect*, he reveals the proven strategies behind those moments of magic. They've captivated television audiences for decades—and they'll work for you too."

—Mark Cornetta, Senior Vice President, TEGNA; President & General Manager, 9NEWS (KUSA/KTVD)

"Steve Spangler helped our entire district kick off a new school year with a powerful message about purpose and engagement. His influence was so profound that we brought him back a few years later to help celebrate our decade-long mission to elevate student engagement. *The Engagement Effect* captures the same energy, insight, and inspiration he brought to our staff—a must-read for any educator or leader committed to meaningful connection."

—Steven Estepp, Superintendent, Mariemont City Schools

"We've had Steve Spangler on stage at the Innovative Schools Summit enough times to know this: He shows up with purpose and delivers every time. He brings engagement, connection, and ideas that stick. *The Engagement Effect* isn't just a book—it's a behind-the-scenes pass to how he does it and why it works."

—Phil Price, President, AccuTrain Corporation

"For over twenty years, I had the pleasure—and occasional peril—of sharing the 9NEWS stage with Steve Spangler. He brought science to life with explosions, laughter, and unforgettable moments, but what really made it great television was the connection he created with viewers. *The Engagement Effect* is the ultimate guide to understanding how he does it."

—Mark Koebrich, Retired Anchor, NBC Affiliate KUSA Denver

"Over seven seasons of the television series *DIY Sci*, Steve Spangler has inspired viewers to roll up their sleeves, ask questions, and create unforgettable memories through hands-on learning. His passion for making STEM education accessible and exciting comes through in every episode—and every page of *The Engagement Effect*. This book is a brilliant guide to designing experiences that connect, captivate, and stick with you long after the experiment is over."

—Steve Rotfeld, President & CEO, Steve Rotfeld Productions

"Whether it was connecting sixteen hundred students through a human circuit or challenging our principals to create their own *best day ever* moments, Steve Spangler showed us that engagement is more than a buzzword—it's a mindset. *The Engagement Effect* is a blueprint for how he thinks, plans, and inspires at the highest level."

—Dr. Kamela Patton, Former Superintendent, Collier County Public Schools

"Steve Spangler is the most powerful motivational speaker I've ever heard. As CEO of Frog Street, we invited Steve to help us transform our annual Splash conference into a truly unforgettable experience. His ability to engage early childhood educators through hands-on learning and powerful storytelling elevated our conference and stimulated educators to strive for greatness. *The Engagement Effect* captures the same energy, strategy, and heart that made Steve's work such a vital part of our community."

—Ron Chase, CEO, Frog Street

"At the American Payroll Association's Annual Congress, we've always believed in creating experiences that educate, connect, and inspire. Steve Spangler brought that vision to life—most memorably when he connected nearly three thousand attendees in a single, electrifying STEM demonstration. *The Engagement Effect* captures the heart of that moment and the strategy behind it. This book is a valuable guide for anyone committed to elevating how people learn and lead."

—Dan Maddux, Executive Director, PayrollOrg (formerly APA)

"Steve's *best day ever* moments have inspired our teachers and administrators to create their own unforgettable moments for students and staff. When one of our principals told me that her teacher had done more hands-on science in three months than she had done in thirty years, I knew we had struck gold with Steve Spangler's approach to engagement. He doesn't just inspire others 'to do'—he inspires them 'to be' the best version of themselves. This book clearly illustrates how he does it and why it matters."

—Ed Short, Former STEM Education Coordinator, Brevard Public Schools

"Steve Spangler's impact on Littleton Public Schools spans over three decades. What began in the classroom has become a legacy of helping educators throughout our district bring learning to life. *The Engagement Effect* is filled with the same strategies and mindset that Steve has shared with our teachers—tools that help create powerful learning experiences and meaningful student connections."

—Dr. Todd Lambert, Superintendent, Littleton Public Schools

CULTIVATING EXPERIENCES

That Ignite Connection, Build Trust, and Inspire Action

THE
ENGAGEMENT
EFFECT

STEVE SPANGLER

Forefront
BOOKS

Published by Forefront Books, Nashville, Tennessee.

Distributed by Simon & Schuster.

Library of Congress Control Number: 2025912367

Print ISBN: 978-1-63763-483-7
E-book ISBN: 978-1-63763-484-4

Cover Design by George Stevens, G Sharp Design LLC
Interior Design by Bill Kersey, Kersey Graphics

Printed in the United States of America

25 26 27 28 29 30 [LAK] 10 9 8 7 6 5 4 3 2 1

Dedication

For Renée,
my North Star—
whose belief in the why gave this book its purpose.
For Jack, Mark, and Scott—
whose curiosity shaped every experience and every page.
For Murphy—
whose frequent need to chase the ball or go for a walk
gave me just enough sanity to finish the book.

CONTENTS

PART 2
THE HARD PART: ENCOURAGING CONNECTION

PART 3
PURPOSE: CULTIVATING ENGAGEMENT

FOREWORD

THERE ARE LEADERS WHO INFORM, AND THERE ARE LEADERS WHO transform. Steve Spangler belongs in that rare category of individuals who do more than just teach—he ignites. His work is a master class in how to cultivate engagement that sparks connection, fosters trust, and ultimately moves people to action.

At High Point University, we believe that learning is most powerful when it's lived—when education becomes an experience, not just a transaction. Steve embodies this philosophy. His work doesn't simply deliver content—it creates moments. Memorable, meaningful, and often magical moments that linger long after the lesson is over.

In *The Engagement Effect*, Steve offers a powerful blueprint for anyone who wants to lead with greater purpose and impact. He draws from a career shaped by the classroom, tested on television, and refined in boardrooms and keynote stages around the world. But at its core, this book is about something deeply human: the art of making people feel seen, valued, and inspired.

Engagement, as Steve teaches, is not a technique—it's a mindset. It's a commitment to being present, to designing experiences that invite participation, and to leading in a way that builds bridges instead of walls. Whether you're an educator, a business leader, or a change-maker of any kind, the insights you'll find here will shift the way you think about influence, connection, and communication.

What makes Steve's message so enduring is its universality. No matter your industry or audience, the principles he shares will help you create experiences that people remember—and, more importantly, experiences that move them to grow. This is not just a book about engagement; it is a call to action for leaders who want to make their impact felt and their presence remembered.

In these pages, Steve Spangler shows us how to harness the Engagement Effect—not by commanding attention, but by earning it through authenticity, generosity, and intentional design. That is the hallmark of transformational leadership.

So, I invite you to turn the page. Not just to read, but to experience. Let this book challenge you, inspire you, and equip you to lead in a way that truly matters.

—Dr. Nido R. Qubein
President, High Point University

INTRODUCTION

FIRE!

THERE'S A REASON WHY I SMELL LIKE LIGHTER FLUID. NO, IT'S NOT cheap cologne. The *eau-de-lighter-fluid* fragrance is a side effect of my morning routine.

Every morning, I wake up, shower, get dressed, load my pockets with the essentials, and then reach for my wallet. It's no ordinary wallet; there're money and credit cards on one side, and on the other, there's a secret compartment that conceals an ignitor device doused in lighter fluid. With the flick of a finger, the sparks ignite the fluid-soaked wick, and the wallet bursts into flames.

Every profession has the "things" they need to do their job. The tools of the trade. Doctors wear a stethoscope, plumbers have wrenches, lawyers have unnecessarily expensive pens . . . and I, the science guy/educator, have the tool I need to measure *engagement*. Here's how it works:

Let's say I'm at Taco Bell ordering a bean burrito. As I open my wallet to pay for my lunch, I secretly trigger the ignitor to make the flames appear.

"Excuse me, would you happen to have any *hot* sauce?" I say nonchalantly.

This is the inflection point, so I'm most interested in what happens next. The flames leap, and the next thing you know, screams of excitement turn into laughter, complete strangers pepper you with questions, and then you hear those three words I've heard thousands of times over the last thirty years:

"Do it again!"

I've also had cups of water thrown on me. It happens.

These reactions all represent different levels of engagement. Consider it real-time data for this engagement scientist. That's my job: I study the science of engagement. Learning how and why people choose to connect and engage unlocks the secret to curiosity and why people lean in to want to learn more. While that may sound like it's just for educators, it's probably even more needed in business as CEOs and managers learn how to engage employees and customers at the highest level. It's why I'm always studying and watching people, and it's why you should consider it too.

There are some pyrotechnics (metaphorical and literal) in these pages. I thought you might want to see some of them, so I've inserted a few QR codes you can scan to take you there without having to search. Use them or ignore them; it's up to you. Look, here comes one now.

My trip to Florence a few years ago provided a data point I wasn't expecting.

No, not that Florence—no cobblestone streets, no Renaissance paintings. I was in Florence, Alabama. I was booked for a keynote presentation before the National Association of Federal Education Program Administrators. They, too, were interested in learning more about the factors that increase student engagement and help the educators they support build even more meaningful connections in the classroom. So they called the science guy.

On travel day, I got up, showered, brushed my teeth, and soaked my wallet in lighter fluid, as always. A few hours later, my wife, Renée, and I landed in Huntsville and rented a car.

After many years on the road as a professional speaker, the routine of checking into a hotel can get a little boring. Name . . . driver's license . . . credit card . . . it's all part of the routine. The trick is to catch the desk clerk at just the right moment. This one looked up from her phone at the last possible second.

"Checking in?"

I took out my wallet as if to grab my credit card while my finger secretly triggered the ignitor. Flames leapt up six inches above my hand.

"Quick question: Do you have anything next to a fire escape?" I said.

I usually give it a two-beat pause before enjoying the moment of surprise. But not this time.

"I don't know," said the woman, expressionless. "I'll have to look."

I've done this thousands of times, and I rarely get crickets.

But this time? Nada. Nothing.

Renée is all too familiar with my hotel check-in routine. She's seen it all—the screams, the laughter, the water—but this time, I got a nonreaction. In fact, I got the opposite of engagement . . . I was in the presence of *disengagement*. I bombed at the front desk.

On the way to the room, I asked Renée, "Did you see the clerk? She gave me *your* 'not funny' look. Maybe she's having a bad day?"

"No, it was you. You rushed it. You didn't give her a chance to connect," she said. "Plus, I think she thought you were trying to *trick* her instead of sharing a fun moment together. Brush it off. Let's go get a cup of coffee."

The next best thing to a hotel clerk is a barista. Summoning flames, followed by a witty comment about *hot* coffee always gets a fun response.

"Would it be possible to make the coffee extra *hot?*"

The barista looked at me *through the flames* and said, "Not really" (punctuated with an eye roll).

We got our coffees and walked back to our room.

"What is going on in Florence, Alabama?" I asked. "I think I'm in for a tough crowd."

As someone who speaks on the science of engagement, I was striking out . . . and my time on stage hadn't even started.

✳

Building connections is my catnip. It's an obsession, which means I'm constantly trying to create experiences to share with those around me. Because shared experience invites connection.

A connection habit can be exhausting for one's spouse, but Renée knew who she was marrying. At restaurants, I catch the attention of a kid sitting in the booth next to us and use sleight of hand to make it look like I'm snorting baby carrots up my nose. We smile at each other. We have a secret. We're suddenly friends, sharing an experience. The world becomes a slightly better place.

The vanishing carrot is the magician part of me; the connection is the human part. But there's a third part, which is probably why you have this book in your hand.

As an educator, my job is to find the most creative ways to make learning fun and meaningful for my students. If I was in a chemistry classroom, I'd trade the carrot trick for gummy bears that spontaneously combust or flash-freeze a banana in a vat of liquid nitrogen and smash it on the desk like the comedian Gallagher to get their undivided attention. Then, I set them up to engage. That's the teacher part. The leader part.

This book is about experience, connection, and engagement. It's about building capacity in other people the way you build static charge on a balloon by rubbing it on your hair. When people are connected and charged up, they are primed to engage.

Engagement doesn't always happen on its own; it needs the right environment to take root. It's not about pushing harder; it's about creating a space where ideas can grow. It thrives in safety, encouragement, freedom, and, above all, connection. As leaders, we create experiences to allow for that connection in the hope that we will see engagement blossom. But no matter how well we lay the groundwork and how hard we hope, we can't force it to happen. People have to choose to engage.

✳

Despite my fears, the keynote in Alabama was really fun. Generally speaking, federal workers are accustomed to a speaker perched behind a podium with a clicker and ninety-seven slides (with really small font). That's why it's fun to catch them off guard with my leaf blower contraption that covers the front row in toilet paper or to keep audience members on their toes as pieces of potato fly through the air. When a spud whizzes past your head at 30 mph, you tend to sit up and listen.

The federal workers connected, and we shared an experience together. We sent them home with Energy Sticks (more about these clever little contraptions later), and about fifty people hung around to tell me about their own experiences of connection and engagement.

But I couldn't shake the wallet fails. Maybe the clerk and the barista saw a slick guy rolling in from Not-the-South, USA, trying to pull one over on them. If people think they are the brunt of your joke . . . they don't like that.

On our last night in Alabama, we had dinner at a local restaurant the hotel had recommended. When we got back, the same stoic woman was at the front desk. She saw me coming. She visibly tensed. I felt terrible.

"Hey," I said. "Do you know Cosmo's Restaurant?"

"Yeah, of course." She's waiting for me to screw with her.

"Best grits I've ever had. I forgot people put shrimp in grits."

She borderline smiled. "Have you never been to the South?"

"We have now. That made our whole trip."

She visibly relaxed, and she looked me in the eye for the first time.

"Thank you for everything," I said.

"I hope y'all have a good trip home."

I knew Alabamians put shrimp in grits. It's delicious. But I felt I had upset this woman, and I don't want to make anybody upset. I just need to connect, and that means creating an experience that leaves room for others to reciprocate that need. That's what went wrong with the wallet. It's what Renée recognized immediately. I had made it about me.

Real connection is a two-way street. It's not just about doing clever things for a laugh or a gasp. It's about crafting an experience, an opportunity for people to play. It should never be about me. It should be about them.

Some techniques work better than others, and nothing works every time. I rarely know why. You can't concoct an algorithm for falling in love—not a decent one, anyway. But after a lifetime of pursuing connection and engagement through experiences, I've seen a lot of things work, and I've seen a lot of things fail.

That's what this book is about: pursuing engagement with those who look to you for leadership, whether it's in a moment or over a lifetime.

A Few Definitions

You may be holding the least prescriptive leadership book on the market, but I want to define a few terms to avoid confusion.

Engagement is forgetting yourself in what you're doing. It is what every teacher dreams of seeing in their students. It is what every true artist experiences in their work. It is what the best businesses in the world encourage in their staff. Cultivating it in others requires a leader to be in every way unselfish, and it will punish those leaders who create false connections to scam or cheat or fool.

Connection is two-way, mutual, and chosen by all parties. No matter how eager to connect you are, no matter how noble your intentions, a one-way handshake is just weird—especially in Alabama. As we will discuss, you have to take your hands off the wheel and hope that someone else will grab it. The path to that connection is shared experience.

Leaders create experiences. Not "sometimes," not "if we choose," and not "when we need engagement." When you are leading, you are creating an experience. If you don't recognize that, you are probably creating a lazy experience. There is showmanship to it. Showmanship is learnable, and every leader needs it.

Leadership is building capacity in another person.

Leadership is building capacity in another person. It is a servant's role, and it is a lot of work. Leaders risk their dignity and the illusion of perfection to create experiences that some people won't like. They do this to encourage connection with the people they lead. If they're lucky, engagement will follow. Magic.

By the way, *magic* is a term you'll see a lot in these pages. Sometimes there's just no better way to emphasize how ... well, *magical* ... an experience can be. So take note whenever you see me drop the "M" word throughout the book. That's not me being repetitive; it's me putting a giant exclamation point on whatever principle I'm talking about.

A Gentle Word of Warning

I have very few hard-and-fast techniques to offer you. The techniques in this book will not encourage subordinates to obey or work harder. In fact, the main focus is what *they* need from *you*. What you *will* find within is what I have seen happen when I do specific things, create certain environments, and invite a particular kind of participation. Some techniques might not work; some may not even be techniques. From those that are, you may be tempted to cherry-pick tactics to help you sell cars or win friends or elections. Be ye warned: It will backfire. Everything in here is booby-trapped. You can use these tactics for selfish gain once, maybe twice. After that, they will smell you coming.

Perhaps I can repel you further.

I'm a science teacher. I've spent part of my career either *as* a teacher or *working with* teachers. And, as you'll see, I've got a million stories about how engagement works (or doesn't) in the education arena.

If you're not a teacher, don't worry—this isn't a book just for educators. In fact, one of the running jokes in education is that most teachers have a side hustle to supplement their "generous" salary. For Renée and me, that side hustle evolved into a series of multimillion-dollar businesses built around educational toys and hands-on science experiences. Renée served as CEO for over twenty-five years, leading a team of forty-five employees and overseeing manufacturing and distribution through overseas partners. Our products made their way into mass-market retailers such as Target, Walmart, and Toys "R" Us. Many of the engagement principles in this book come directly from those experiences with vendors, customers, and our own team. This dual perspective—from classroom to boardroom—shapes the way we think about engagement and brings a broader relevance to the lessons you'll explore in the chapters ahead.

I've spent the past several years speaking to more and more corporate audiences—from sandwich chains to payroll professionals—and I've discovered something that blew my mind: The engagement principles that capture students' attention in the classroom are the same principles that capture the CEO's attention in the boardroom.

Anytime I talk about engagement, I find I can substitute the word *teacher* with the word *leader*. Is that because your employees are big children? No. It's because idiosyncratic, individual children comprise the experience of a classroom exactly as idiosyncratic, individual employees comprise the experience of an office. If you don't respect them as individuals, you will fail. And they will eat you alive.

✳

A lot of people ask me for the engagement recipe. That's how I tricked my publisher into publishing this book. Here's the closest thing I have:
1. Leaders create shared experiences.

2. Shared experiences allow for real connection.
3. Real connection breeds engagement.

Everyone is in a leadership role at some time or another, even if it's driving a taxi, taking someone on a date, presenting the Q2 spending report, or hosting Thanksgiving dinner. Every experience is different, but the feeling of connection and the architecture of engagement are basically the same, even in a passing interaction at a check-in desk, through a screen, or in a classroom. That's true even if the engagement happens years later when someone is alone at their desk.

Creating connections with people, even strangers, has been my life's work. As with anything, if you do it long enough, you get good at it. It has taken me from birthday-party magic shows to science on an A/V cart to keynotes for thousands of kids, teachers, STEM experts, and payroll professionals (really) to four billion views on YouTube. It took me to *The Ellen DeGeneres Show* twenty-seven times and has us on season eight of my second nationally syndicated series, which is called *DIY Sci* as of this writing.

That might sound braggy, but my point is that I have practiced and practiced and practiced, so I have lots of examples of what works and what doesn't. You will find those here, in mostly bite-sized portions with some bigger bites mixed in.

There are days when I never get a chance to light the wallet and see a surprised expression. It doesn't mean the lighter fluid went to waste; it just means there wasn't an opportunity to engage and connect. That's OK. It was still worth it. At least I juiced it, and I was ready to go.

The pursuit of experience, connection, and engagement is a *habit*, one that improves every aspect of my life every day—and that's because it is fundamentally about improving other people's lives first.

PART 1

THE FUN PART: CRAFTING EXPERIENCES

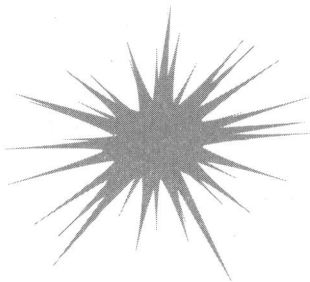

CHAPTER 1

YOU ARE THE MAESTRO, LIKE IT OR NOT

GREW UP IN A FAMILY OF MAGICIANS. THAT IS NOT A METAPHOR. MY parents were professional, working magicians. We owned tuxedos. We bought playing cards by the pallet. The house was littered with fancy-looking boxes stuffed with silk handkerchiefs. My mom climbed into a box, and my dad cut her into three pieces. You get the idea.

My dad went to school to be a chemist. He didn't want to be in a lab, so he chose to be an electrical engineer, but chemistry still played into absolutely everything. Our kitchen also doubled as a lab of sorts, and that's where my dad invented the fake blood that was used by special effects artists in the movies. KISS and Penn & Teller used his fake blood on stage in the 1970s because it looked so good. My dad was a great chemist, and he used his wizardry to invent magic tricks still used by famous magicians today. Imagine holding what looks like an ordinary glass of water, but on command the water turns jet black. It's so startling that people have been known to drop the glass.

"Dad, how do you make the water turn black?"

"I can't teach you that until you study acids and bases *when*—not *if*—you take chemistry. Once you learn something about the pH scale, let me know."

Eventually, this clever man realized he was unhappy in the grind of the corporate machine. That's when my mom told him to go for it with magic, and he did. They traveled the country doing magic shows and speaking at conferences, and Dad worked as a magic consultant from home in Denver. Yes, he was a magic consultant—for some pretty famous magicians, in fact . . . as well as those not-so-famous working professionals you might see at a kid's party or a corporate event. Even a kid who called himself David Copperfield dropped by the house to work out a trick or two with my dad.

When a group of magicians get together, it's just like what happens when a group of teachers or corporate types get together: They drink and talk shop.

"I got booked for the halftime show at a basketball game, and they want me to make the cheerleaders disappear."

Never, in all my years of sitting on the sideline and watching these meetings of the mind from afar, did I ever hear the magicians say, "That's impossible." Instead, I heard, "OK, let's think on that." Then, they would work backward. They always solved the problem backward—from the reveal to the setup. Outcome first, then solution.

That was one of many valuable lessons I picked up in the informal magical society of my youth.

The most important of those lessons was the art of engagement.

If you're a magician booked to do table-to-table magic at a restaurant, the most important part of your show isn't the tricks; it's the way you approach the table. Most people would rather continue their dinner conversation than see a card trick. The secret is to find a creative, nonthreatening, engaging way to approach the table. Let's face it: It's hard to compete with spaghetti.

What's your desired outcome in this scenario? The lowest imaginable bar is they don't ask you to leave, no one throws anything at you, and the kids don't cry. A little higher is a moment of glory for you, the pimple-faced magician on his first restaurant gig. But what if you aim for something truly elevated—what if you *provide* something: a shared experience between magician and diners that creates a connection and leaves them transformed?

If that's your objective, the energy of the experience shifts from you to them. Suddenly, things start clicking. You acknowledge them as people, and they acknowledge you right back. You're attentive to them, and they lean in. You ask instead of telling, and they answer instead of nodding. You've connected. They're in. Spaghetti forgotten.

> **If you're a leader, you're in the experience business, the connection business, the engagement business.**

You're a teacher in charge of twenty-seven fourth graders. You're a barista at a busy coffee shop. You're CEO of a tech giant. You're the self-proclaimed emperor of a secessionist island nation. If you're a leader, you're in the experience business, the connection business, the engagement business. You are the maestro. The first step in achieving that outcome is creating a shared experience, which has a lot to do with showmanship.

If your goal is to get by or to enjoy some glory, you've got the wrong job (and the wrong book). When you approach leadership as service to those around you and you seek connection as a means to engagement and transformation . . . every environment is elevated.

Our goal as teachers, leaders, and magicians is to build capacity in those who follow us by designing experiences that foster connection and invite engagement. That's your outcome. Shifting your mindset is a great first step. But pulling it off takes practice.

The Lesson

- Leaders are always creating an experience. Whether you mean to or not, you're crafting an emotional environment. Be deliberate.
- Connection comes before engagement. When you create a shared moment, the audience leans in—and that's when the real magic begins.
- Outcome first, then solution. Like the magicians in the basement, work backward from the kind of connection you want to create.
- Showmanship isn't a gimmick; it's a skill. Every leader needs it. Learn it. Practice it.

CHAPTER 2

HAVE YOUR ACT TOGETHER

THE FIRST TIME I REMEMBER SEEING MY PARENTS WORK, I WAS standing in the wings of the Paramount Theater in Denver, and Dad was cutting Mom into three pieces. Mom climbed into the box. Dad slid in the blades and pulled off her center section. Mom beamed. People clapped. I was five.

This was at a time when there was a real orchestra in the pit below the stage. The musicians sort of came with the theaters; they were part of the package. But there was very little rehearsal with each orchestra. They knew in advance what to play and when to play it, but that was about it. Mom got chopped up while the orchestra played "Breaking Up Is Hard to Do," and then to finish the show, the orchestra played "Granada" while Mom and Dad ate fire. Magic.

The act was called Magic Moments, and my parents performed it all over the country. It was elaborate, and a whole lot happened, but Magic Moments was a tight twenty-two minutes. I saw it a thousand times, and I watched what happened to the audience over the course of that twenty-two minutes. I got to be backstage for all the inter-action with the other magicians on the bill, and then I got to watch their sets too.

There were three lessons I remember absorbing from the Magic Moments tours.

Lesson 1: Be Human

Dad looked the part of a magician and Mom was pretty, neither of which hurts when you're trying to get an audience's attention. But even better, they didn't hide the fact that they were a married couple. It humanized them instantly; the audience started looking for interpersonal dynamics as soon as they knew these two were sleeping together. Magic Moments was a formal affair of gowns and tuxes, but the marriage aspect gave Mom and Dad a living-room humanity that the solo acts had to work for. Being recognizably human is instantly disarming, even if you're sawing your spouse in half.

Lesson 2: Keep It Tight

Once a performer's act hits the thirty-minute mark, they almost always lose the audience. Some of the solo acts were irresistibly lovable. Others had to squander time to build rapport with the audience. But even when the lovable ones hit the thirty-minute mark, the squeak of a seat, the sound of a door closing in the back of the theater, or even a whisper from the shadows told the same story: The magician had overstayed their welcome.

The Spanglers were smart. Twenty-two minutes gave the audience time to get to know them, like them, and invest in them—but still miss them when they were gone. My parents got them hooked, kept it tight, and left them satisfied, even if they could have taken another trick. You're borrowing someone's time when they trust you with an experience. Don't squander it.

Lesson 3: Maintain Control

A less-than-wonderful orchestra could ruin a whole show. If their timing was off, or if they played the sawing song during the banter and the pretty song during the fire-eating, all was lost. If the violins were out of tune, forget about it. Mom and Dad still performed the act seamlessly, but I knew it would be a quiet dinner that night.

Today, the most likely element to go wrong is technology. Sometimes, during keynotes, I show a video in which a thousand kids join hands over a few acres of land to allow electrons to pass through them, complete a circuit, and trigger a noisemaker. But if we haven't maintained enough control over whatever ballroom I'm speaking in, sometimes there's no sound—which diminishes the thrill of a noisemaker, and the point is lost.

I always include this part toward the middle-end of the keynote for just this reason: I've worked hard to build rapport with the audience, they're eager to forgive if things go awry, and I've got enough runway left to recover and keep things moving. I can get past it, but there's no way to spin a tech malfunction as intentional, same as the detuned orchestra. It's a distraction.

✳

These three lessons boil down to the same thing: Have your act together. Creating a transformative experience (or even a pleasant one) requires some thought, some work, and maybe some infrastructure. If I don't juice up the fire wallet in the morning, that thing's not going to ignite.

There's no such thing as complete control, so having your act together also means practice. One reason an English teacher in her twenty-fifth year is good at teaching *Hamlet* is that she's taught it twenty-five times. She knows to leave a full day for Act 3, Scene 1, so the sophomores can speculate on what Hamlet and Ophelia have been up to offstage.

When you are creating an experience—a presentation, a science experiment, a keynote, a quick speech at the PTO meeting—preparation will keep it tight and relaxed. Know your apparatus but stay quick on your feet. That will allow both you and those you are leading to focus on your experience together instead of on the out-of-tune violins.

The Lesson

- Be human. Don't hide your quirks—they might just be your connection point.
- Keep it tight. Leave your audience wanting more, not checking their watches.
- Control what you can. When the A/V tech flubs it, your preparation is your safety net.
- Rehearsal isn't optional. Practice frees you up to focus on people, not problems.

CHAPTER 3

PROXIMITY

"**S**TEVEN, TELL US SOMETHING ABOUT YOUR MOM AND DAD."

I was sitting crisscross-applesauce on the rug of my kindergarten classroom. Mrs. Carden and my peers were watching me intently.

"My dad saws my mom into three pieces," I said. "Then they eat fire."

My peers were incredulous, disgusted by my sheer audacity to tell such an incredible lie in school. Mrs. Carden also didn't buy it.

"Jenny, tell us something about *your* mom and dad."

But Little Steven had something going for him: It was 1972—and back then, safety was merely an afterthought.

The next week, my dad came to school with the torches. He ate fire on the same rug in Mrs. Carden's kindergarten. Magic.

Who cares *what* Jenny's dad does? If your dad eats fire, you are the coolest kid in class.

"How did he do that?"

"Does your dad eat fire all the time?"

"Can *you* eat fire?"

If your dad eats fire, you are the coolest kid in class.

I'm known for soliciting help from the audience during most of my presentations. One of my favorite pieces of audience participation is a signature routine I do with a dozen eggs and a tray of glasses. It's a piece that requires a little skill and lots of guts to pull off in front of a large audience. I never know who I'm going to pick until the speech has begun because I need some time to read the room, watch body language, and look for someone who I think will be coachable on stage. But every single time, the first question that person gets asked when they return to their seat is, "Were you in on it? Did you know he would pick you? How did you know how to knock the eggs into the glasses?"

Teachers have executed this maneuver since time immemorial. Sometimes, they let the future valedictorian clean the chalkboard or run notes to the office—because it means the world to them. But the clever ones deputize the girl with the wandering attention, the stoic who needs coaxing out of his shell, or the troublemaker carrying problems from home. Bosses can abuse their power by adopting pets, but they can also create an experience around each special project by deputizing employees one at a time. People feel special when they're *made* to feel special. Even if it's basic, they feel valued when their expertise is requested. The best leaders quickly discover—if they'll just take their hands off the wheel—that their employees are actually truly helpful and supersmart.

"We have to inventory the warehouse for the first time in a decade. Your knowledge of our old product is the best in the office. Can we do this one together?"

"I've got to write something for the university newsletter. Would you mind looking over a few drafts as I finish them? I trust your editing."

This is good stuff, and it's all about proximity and trust. When you shrink the distance between the stage and the house, people are going to connect, and then they're going to engage. Your deputized editor is going to feel proud of that newsletter, even if your name is the only one on the byline. Though I ask you, Fearless Leader: Would it kill your pride to put their name on it as well?

✳

I did not eat fire in kindergarten; it would be decades before I tasted the flame. But I was close to somebody who did. I saw the reaction Dad got from my friends and the way my friends talked to me about it. I got to be cool because my dad ate fire.

As the leader, you are a fire-eater. But your superpower isn't eating fire; it's making those who follow you the coolest kids in class.

The Lesson

- Pull people into the experience. Deputize them. Invite them to be part of the magic.
- People want to feel seen, special, and needed. Use proximity and trust to turn spectators into participants.
- You don't have to be the fire-eater. Sometimes just standing near one is enough to ignite someone's curiosity.

CHAPTER 4

PRACTICE THE STORY PART

M Y DAD GAVE ME MY FIRST MAGIC TRICK WHEN I WAS FIVE YEARS old. It was the cups and the balls. You put a ball in one cup, you stack all three cups, and the ball magically appears in a different cup. Magic. It's a simple trick to learn.

I remember Dad presenting it to me.

"We don't show anybody the trick, Steven, until we've practiced. You will show me first, and I'll tell you when you're ready to show somebody else. You don't just go and show your friends your magic trick."

When I had the trick down, I performed it for Dad.

"That's good," Dad said. "But you didn't get my attention."

"But I made the ball change cups."

"What are you going to *say*?" he asked. "What story are you going to make up?"

A story? I spent a week getting the cups and the balls down cold, and now I had to invent a story? I thought I was just doing a trick. I went back to my room.

The story I came up with was that I always forgot which cup I put the ball in. I'd put it in the first cup and stack them where the audience could see it.

"Shoot, I forgot where I put the ball again. Did anyone see?"

"The first one! It's in the first one!"

"Are you sure? I feel like I put it in the second one. This is so confusing."

It made a tight little narrative. When Dad was satisfied, he green-lighted the trick, and I was ready for show-and-tell. It was a big deal. I woke up extra early that morning.

Maybe it was nerves, maybe it was rebellion, but I decided to skip the story. It felt forced. I'll just go up and do the trick. Knock 'em dead. I flopped.

"I saw the ball! The ball is in your hand!"

When you're five years old, and you flop in front of your friends, you feel it. I was embarrassed and demoralized, and I knew I'd have to tell Dad what happened. Mainly, I knew I really just had to workshop the story.

It was in the workshopping that I realized the story was so much more powerful than the sleight of hand. I could do the trick, but people connected through the story. In fact, the sleight of hand worked way, way better as an appendage to the story. And not just because it was a distraction. In a kindergarten-sized way, the story turned the spotlight on the audience, which transformed an experience into connection and engagement.

✳

I had been doing monthly magic tricks for about half the school year when I busted Mrs. Carden acting confused about something she was teaching us. She may have even used my line: "I always forget . . . can you help me?"

She stole my bit! I was decades away from being a good showman, let alone a good teacher or leader, but Dad and Mrs. Carden had given me a glimpse at what lay beyond the razzle-dazzle of magic tricks. At the time, all I knew was that the stories made my tricks come off better. What I would discover later (when I had a higher purpose than the cup-and-ball trick) was that I could invite connection and engagement the same way. But I had more lessons ahead of me first.

The Lesson

- The story matters more than the trick. Sleight of hand will amaze, but story is what connects.
- Crafting a narrative invites your audience into the experience. That's where engagement happens.
- If you want them to remember the moment, give them a story to hold on to.

CHAPTER 5

THEY HAVE TO LIKE YOU FIRST

AGIC CLUBS ARE A REAL THING—MAGICIANS GETTING TOGETHER once a month to share tricks. It's a great way to pick up new illusions and practice your craft. It's also a good excuse to get out of your parents' basement for a few hours.

It was the third Thursday of the month, and during my early teens that could only mean one thing: magic meeting night! I walked in off the street, snow still piled on my shoulders, and some twenty-year-old came up and asked me to "pick a card, any card." All I wanted to do was find the bathroom and maybe fortify myself with a crappy cup of coffee, but here I was, staring down the barrel of the worst kind of card-sharp stereotype.

Who the heck is this guy anyway?

After my second coffee, I bought the kid a Shirley Temple and told him a hard truth about creating an experience: No matter how smooth the trick is, I'm not going to engage if you don't give me a chance to like you. I don't even know you, and you're trying to impress me with your card skills. You want my attention, but it's not working the way you'd hoped because I'm irritated, so I'm *burning your hands*—that's magician speak for *watching what you're doing*, trying to catch the trick.

"I saw you do the top change. I saw you do the double lift and the false shuffle."

"What? How? Why?"

"Because there was nothing else for me to do. All you gave me was a trick, so all I could focus on was the trick. Also, I didn't like you yet, so I was eager to catch you."

It's Not About the Trick

This was kindergarten all over again, but it was different in one significant way. In Mrs. Carden's class, the kids already knew me. I needed a story to bring them in, but I didn't have to make introductions. If I like you first and you pull me in, then the magic just seems to happen.

I tried to communicate this to the card-trick kid that night.

"Let's find somebody else in here," I said. "You're going to do the same trick, but I'm going to make up a story first. Just let me talk and follow my lead."

I found a lady with a kind face whose coffee, I suspected, was Irish.

"Excuse me, ma'am," I said. "We need you to settle something. My friend thinks he can sense the heat from your hand on playing cards. He thinks people use that to cheat at poker. I can't do it because I just came from outside, and my hands are freezing. Could we use yours?"

"Yeah, sure." She was interested. She felt needed. She was in.

"Great. Thanks."

The kid did his trick. She picked a card, and he did a little *abracadabra* in keeping with the story about the heat.

"It was the eight of hearts," he said. Magic.

"Whoa!"

This lady may have been half-sauced, but she was no fool. She realized this was a magic trick, not an experiment. We *were* in a magic club, after all. But she was delighted because the approach was different right from the start. These goofy guys were having a silly disagreement, and they needed her to arbitrate. She wasn't just a ritual sacrifice; she was involved, she was part of the trick, and most importantly, she liked us.

"That was so good," she said. "You really had me. Can you do another one? Let me get my friend."

Boom. She liked him. He was in. Whenever you hear the phrases "Do it again!" or "Can you show my friend?" you know you've made a connection.

I slid into the shadows, leaving my grateful new friend to impress the pair of lovely ladies who were now laser-focused on him.

✳

Here's the bad news if, by chance, you're looking for a prescriptive way to make them like you: You've got to like *them* first.

Here's the bad news if, by chance, you're looking for a prescriptive way to make them like you: You've got to like *them* first.

I don't make the rules; I'm just telling you how it works. If you try to make people like you without respecting them as human beings worthy of being liked, you are being a creep. If you don't like people or if you're so entrenched in ambition that you see people as either a means or an obstacle, it's time to make a change in your thinking. Otherwise, leadership might not be for you.

That's not to say that narcissists aren't frequently "successful" leaders. They are—momentarily . . . and maybe monetarily. But they leave a trail of bodies behind them and a lot of burnt bridges. They create experiences based on paranoia and fear. Eventually, their humanity is hard to identify.

A pack of cards can be a catalyst for a conversation that would've never taken place otherwise. The truth of the experience is not about the trick. It's *never* about the trick. It's about the conversation, the two-way connection that takes place when people are present to each other and giving as much love as they take. I don't want to see a magic trick from someone who disdains me. I'll have one foot out the door before the cards are shuffled, no matter how cold it is.

The Lesson

- Likability precedes engagement. They need to trust you before they'll buy into anything you're offering.
- The trick isn't the trick. Connection beats cleverness every time.
- If you want people to like you, start by genuinely liking them first. There's no shortcut.

CHAPTER 6

FIFTEEN SECONDS

WHEN YOU'RE DOING TABLE-TO-TABLE MAGIC AT A RESTAURANT, you've got about fifteen seconds for people to either engage or tell you to scram. Even for a great magician, the first couple of tables are always tough, because you've got to get the buzz going.

You slide up to a family of five, tell them the kitchen sent you with a question about their order, and segue into a quick trick. The kids like it, the parents are relieved their order is safe, and you get in and out. Do that a couple of times, maybe throw in something with an open flame, and soon, a buzz is happening in the room.

People are asking their waiter or waitress, "Is the guy gonna come to our table?" The engagement is perfect because the connection has already been made—*from across the room.*

How did you do that? You didn't. They did. You just invited them. You created a safe space for them to choose to connect. That is an effective experience.

*

Science is a way harder sell than magic. Very few people want to sit and learn about particle theory, especially over lasagna. Shout-out to those who do, but you are a small minority.

When I started doing elementary school assemblies right after college, I had no idea how to capture the attention of a hundred first graders. They will subsume and devour you in forty-five painful minutes. I never took a master's-level course on classroom management, but after thirteen years on the road and with forty-five hundred school assemblies under my belt, I think I could teach one.

Magic shows had taught me to set expectations at the very beginning—within fifteen seconds. You can't walk out in front of a hundred kids and go, "Let me tell you a little bit about myself." You can't do that. Instead, while the principal's introducing me, I ignite my flaming book from behind her. (Yes, I sometimes trade the flaming wallet for a flaming book. Anything worth doing is worth overdoing.)

Anything worth doing is worth overdoing.

"Boys and girls, today's speaker is Steve Spangler . . ."

Meanwhile, my book goes aflame in the background. The kids scream "Agh!" and the principal's like, "I asked you to stay quiet." I close the book. The principal doesn't know that I'm doing this. I look at the kids and mime *Shhh*. When she starts speaking again, I open the book and light it up, and the kids lose their minds.

I've got them at this point. Fifteen seconds. They're experiencing something they've never seen, they're involved in the conspiracy, and they'll be engaged in what I tell them if I keep the energy up and the surprises coming.

As for the principal, she was in on the plot before we even started. This makes her part of the big show, and she gets to take credit for a memorable opening. It's also a great strategy to get invited back.

After the show, a few teachers inevitably come to speak to me.

"Where did you teach?" they say. "Have you read Harry Wong's book on classroom management skills?"

"I've never seen a speaker keep two hundred kids' attention like this."

Teachers get it.

Later in my career, I would use that conversation to say, "You should come take our summer course. There's a whole bunch of cool things we can learn together. I didn't do anything that hard." But for the first few years, all I knew was what worked. And what worked was the fifteen-second countdown. Well . . . that and being the bad boy.

✳

As a leader, you're a performer—like it or not—and the show starts before the show starts. When you've only got fifteen seconds to get the attention you need for an experience, it pays to stay a step or two (or three) ahead of everyone.

The Lesson

- You have fifteen seconds to get their attention. Make it count.
- Surprise, delight, or intrigue—but never bore. The window closes fast.
- Set the tone immediately. Don't wait to be interesting.

CHAPTER 7

SEQUENCING

I WAS IN WASHINGTON, DC, AT A NATIONAL SPEAKERS ASSOCIATION conference a few years ago, and a woman named Immaculée Ilibagiza changed the hearts of fifteen hundred people simultaneously.

Immaculée moved the room differently than any speaker I'd ever heard, and she did it through a harrowing yet inspiring story of survival and forgiveness. She chronicled her experience hiding in a tiny bathroom for ninety-one days during the Rwandan genocide. She lost her family but found strength through her faith, ultimately choosing to forgive her perpetrators and become a powerful advocate for peace and reconciliation.

For me, Immaculée's story itself was incredibly difficult and affecting. This amazing woman brought a light and energy to the entire room that you felt whether you knew what was happening or not.

I was sitting next to two good friends. They were sobbing openly. *Everybody* was sobbing openly. A speech's greatness is not measured in tears, but the way Immaculée transformed that room, and that moment was so astonishing and complete that tears were inevitable. Everyone in attendance went through an intense experience with her, and when she was done, we were all heaps of emotion.

Immaculée bowed to a standing ovation, and we all collapsed into our chairs, more puddles than people.

Next up on the big program . . . they brought up a sports guy. A rah-rah guy. No break. No breath. This poor guy had the fear of God in his eyes as he bounced up to the microphone like we'd just finished a commercial break and said, "Let me tell you a joke."

We couldn't deal with it. We were dead to him. There was no room in our hearts for rah-rah. We couldn't even process what he was saying.

Let me be clear: It was not his fault. He was a great speaker with content that was meaningful and fun. But our emotional sponge was already soaked and couldn't absorb anything else.

Immaculée had allowed us to create an experience in ourselves, and she did that by giving us room in *her* story, an African woman's story. She delivered it such that we, mostly white American men and women, could see ourselves in it. That's the greatest feat any storyteller can pull off, and she did it in a way that felt so effortless that it took my breath away.

The emcee for the morning should have come out and said, "What an amazing thing we all just experienced. There's fresh coffee for you. We're going to come back in twenty minutes and change things up."

But they brought up the sports guy. Immediately. He didn't have a chance.

✳

Sometimes I open keynotes with a bit using toilet paper and a leaf blower. It's super visual and super fun. Can you imagine if I had been up next with that? I would have hidden under a pile of coats until everybody went home.

Arbitrary sequencing is rolling the dice in the most dangerous way. In a realized experience, there are no isolated, discrete elements. Everything flows from and to everything else, just like a beautiful multicourse meal. There's a reason those don't begin with brandy and chocolate lava cake.

Be deliberate in your sequencing. And next time you have a drink, pour one out for the sports guy.

The Lesson

- Timing is everything. Sequence can make or break the experience.
- Stacking the right emotional beats in the right order creates transformation.
- Read the room and give people space when they need it.

CHAPTER 8

WHEN THEY DON'T LIKE YOU

OUR TRASH COLLECTOR DOESN'T CARE FOR ME. I GO OUT AND TRY TO help him load the trash. He hates that. But I can't help myself.

I recently left him a giant bag of candy bars with a little note: "Hey, thanks for all you do." He picked up the trash that day, as usual. When I went out to get the can, the candy was gone. The next trash day, I was waiting for him.

"Hey, man. Did you get the candy?"

"Yeah," he said, no eye contact. "I put it in the cab."

No thank-you. No connection. No nothing.

"You work so hard. You need extra energy," I said.

"Uh-huh."

Nothing. Not getting him. But I like to think it messed with him for the rest of the day.

✳

Why do I care about the trash guy? Because he's going to have an awakening. He may never like me, but one day he's going to realize that he is worth being interested in.

By way of clarification, this is not a religious, evangelical thing. I'm not trying to tell him about Jesus or the Qur'an or the Church of Steve. But I've seen what happens when people make that personal discovery, and I want that for the garbage man.

That said, you can try too hard to win a person over. There is always the possibility that I'm just not going to resonate with someone, as much as I want to connect. Sometimes, people just aren't ready, or they're in a moment of crisis, or they've been burned before. You can't force them to connect.

You can't force them to connect.

The Energy Stick is a science toy I invented and marketed in 2011 to teach the concepts of simple circuit building and conductivity and to help kids classify materials as insulators or conductors of electricity.

Here's how the Energy Stick works: If I grab one end and they grab the other, nothing happens because we didn't complete the electrical circuit. If we do the same thing and I touch their sweater with my free hand, still nothing happens because the sweater isn't a conductor of electricity. But if we join free hands, skin touching skin, we complete the circuit, providing a path for the electrons to flow. The LED lights flash, the gizmo makes a noise, and the "aha" moment happens: The sweater is an insulator, and your skin is a conductor.

What are the insulators in your life that prevent you from making a meaningful, mutual connection? It's a decent metaphor.

The only time I've ever heard of the Energy Stick not working was in Nairobi, Kenya. Kerry Kerrigan is a teacher from Steamboat, Colorado, who attended our summer STEM institute in the late 2000s. She volunteered to help teach children in Kenya as part of the Classroom without Walls program.

As Kerry told the story, the classroom was a hut with dirt floors. The students huddled around her to see the "magic" that kept appearing from her bag of tricks. While she tried to teach scientific principles, each activity took on a magical quality. She saved the Energy Stick for the big finale. A group of about twenty children held hands, and two of them added the Energy Stick to complete the human circuit. But it didn't work. She checked to make sure everyone was holding hands . . . the connections were solid, but the stick didn't light up or buzz. When she tried it by herself, the darn thing worked. Not a great finale, but the students seemed to enjoy their time with the "magic lady."

Later that day, the headmaster solved the riddle of the Energy Stick that didn't work.

"It's water. The children get their ration of water once a day at lunchtime. That's why your stick trick didn't work. Their skin is too dry to conduct the electrical charge. You should try it again when they return from lunch," he said.

Bingo. It worked.

When Kerry shared the story with us, she used the lesson as a reminder that just because you're holding hands doesn't mean you're connected with someone. It also illustrated in the starkest terms that there are certain basic needs that must be met before a human being can reach their potential. It would behoove us all to remember that the water we drink isn't just necessary for life; it's necessary for growth and connection with others.

In terms of pure science, the electrons need a path to flow to complete the circuit. Without moisture in the skin, the electrons can't flow. To build a connection, you need a healthy path for information and emotions. Kerry used the metaphor to highlight the need for children to come to school with food and drink in their bellies. Before we can teach them, our students need to be ready to learn. Powerful lesson.

Take a minute to relate this to your life and the people with whom you've tried to connect but failed. Just as water provided the moisture needed to carry the electrons around the circle of children, there's something missing from the connection in your situation. Every relationship and encounter is unique; there's no one-size-fits-all answer. But my hope is that this thought stays with you during those difficult times when you're frustrated by a seemingly unforgeable connection: Someone isn't ready, and it's probably not their fault. Be patient, be kind, and stay available.

It's Not About You

When you're standing around at your thirty-year class reunion, drinking box wine from a plastic cup, a version of this conversation is going to play out:

"Hey, remember Ms. Arnold?"

"Yeah, she was horrible."

"Seriously? She's the reason I got an English degree."

Same thing with a movie. Everybody doesn't leave the theater feeling the same way. We had the same experience—we sat in the same theater, and we watched the same frames scroll by—but we didn't connect likewise. We couldn't. We're all too different.

I know I must come to grips with the fact that I can't connect and engage with everyone I meet. For someone like me, that's easier said than done. But I've learned to back off a little bit—garbage man notwithstanding—and I've learned to teach teachers and managers and anyone else who will listen to back off sometimes too. It's the only way a kid can choose to fully connect. It's also the only way they can choose to barely connect. Celebrate that every time! But remember that sometimes they will choose to wall off. If you're giving them the space they need, it's pretty much never about you.

The Time It Was About Me

I woke up one morning, filled my to-go cup with coffee, and pointed the car toward an elementary school in Denver. This was the era of my speaking and teaching career when I was on the school assembly circuit. I had a tight fifty-minute presentation I would do three to five times a day, so I could engage with students in smaller groups. (I learned early in my career that cramming five hundred kids and teachers into a gym with a horrible sound system was like watching an amoeba engulf food in the middle of a petri dish.)

The show was called "Making Science Fun," and judging from the laughter and applause, I think it went pretty well. The kids freaked out at all the moments I hoped they would: flying potatoes, the static-electricity machine, smoke rings appearing from the trash can . . . the whole thing.

But there was a teacher in the audience who gave me the stinkiest stink-eye that ever stunk. It was the look your mom gave you when you were bad in church. I got that look from this teacher the whole time I was doing my thing. In all the programs I had done—over forty-five hundred at that point—I had never gotten anything like that before. Clearly, something was wrong.

My tummy told me to go talk to her. So, at the very end of the program, while the principal was addressing the couple hundred kids who were in the audience, I snuck around to the back of the gym and approached the not-so-happy teacher.

"Excuse me, ma'am?" I said. "I'm sorry, but I think I may have offended you."

"Yes, you did," she said. "You come in here with your little box of tricks and jokes and silly experiments, and the kids laugh and clap. You get them all fired up, and by the end, they're on their feet clapping like they've just seen the greatest show on earth."

"Yes, ma'am?" I said with a little apprehension in my voice.

"I've been here twenty-two years. I'm a hardworking teacher. The kids do well in my class. But in all those years, I've never gotten a standing ovation. This is hard work. It's not a circus or a game."

It slapped me in the face, and it made me reflect. I stood there stunned for what seemed like an eternity, though I'm sure it was just a few seconds. Then I thanked her for giving me something to think about, and I packed up my stuff and headed to the car.

I hadn't brought anything special to the school that day. My trunk was full of common household stuff you could use to do some pretty fun experiments. That's part of the secret. Audiences connect with my content faster when they see me using items they could find at home. But what had I left the teachers with? Kids who were hyped and ready—but no suggestions about what they, the day-in-and-day-out teachers, could do with that energy. The stink-eye teacher was right: I got the kids all riled up, and then I sent them back to class.

After forty-five hundred school programs performing science for kids, I came home to Renée that night and said, "I think I'm done with that."

That's when my work changed from being a science evangelist traveling from school to school to offering professional development experiences for teachers. I had connected with tens of thousands of students all over the country in bursts of shared experience. During those thirteen years on the road, I learned a lot about strategies to connect with students—how to craft experiences that grab kids by the collar and make them want to learn more. I might have earned a PhD in student engagement strategies if only someone was giving those out. Those years taught me hard and rewarding lessons I continue to use to this very day. But it was time to hang up the well-crafted "kid show" and dig deep to come up with a way to share what I had learned with teachers who wanted to connect and engage with their students at a higher level.

The Lesson

- Not everyone will connect with you. That's OK.
- Connection needs a clear path. Sometimes people just aren't ready. It's not about you.
- Give people space to choose to connect. That's where real engagement lives.
- If you want to grow, listen to the tough feedback...then evolve.

CHAPTER 9

IN SEARCH OF THE SCIENCE
OF ENGAGEMENT

YOU MAY FIND, AS I HAVE, THAT STUDYING THE HARD SCIENCE OF engagement is something of a scavenger hunt. I get overwhelmed fast, which is usually when I consult an expert if I can find one. Dr. Amy Holcombe is dean of the Stout School of Education at High Point University. She is an expert in teacher effectiveness and education leadership. I asked Dr. Holcombe why I couldn't find much in the way of hard research into the science of what I call engagement. She didn't hesitate with her explanation.

"It's disguised as other things," she said. "For instance, ideas around community and communities of practice; you'll find engagement science there. You might look at the concept of belonging; that's another place you'll find it. And restorative practices; you'll find engagement there too."

Should I listen to my smart friends? I should. But I wanted apples-to-apples comparisons. I wanted someone to tell me about the *real* science of engagement, and I wanted them to use those terms. Thus began a confusing quest.

Human Resource Development (HRD)

Human Resource Development was where I struck pay dirt, or so I thought. Articles on engagement from practical and empirical angles populated my ProQuest search, many peppered with that most fascinating word: *neuroscience*.

Surprisingly—to me, anyway—the HR research I found was more preoccupied with *harnessing* employee engagement than *inspiring* it. In this context, engagement was defined as "the cognitive, emotional, and behavioral energy an employee directs toward positive organizational outcomes."[1] A little stiff, but that's not a crime. What bothered me was that it defined engagement in terms of its impact on the organization, not on the employee. It was as if the inspiration, momentum, and care I see in cases of highest engagement only mattered if they were then reinvested into corporate goals. It sounded to me like the quest for a more tempting carrot and a more stinging stick.

If I'm being generous, I'd say these scholars and I are talking about two different things. If I'm being *honest* . . . when I read that definition, I did a spit take and screamed, "That's not engagement!" Hot coffee dribbled down my shirt. The dog hid under the table.

I knew how to get a classroom full of kids or a conference hall full of educators to connect with an experience and, hopefully, engage. I wasn't looking for a recipe—I had that, or as close as I could come (you're reading it). I was looking for an explanation. Why did some antics work while others didn't? What was going on in the brain? Gimme some science!

For this educator, *engagement* is the code word for selfless victory.

For this educator, *engagement* is the code word for selfless victory. Engagement in a student will sustain them in their personal journey but make little measurable impact on the school or the teacher who encouraged it (except perhaps for their feelings of satisfaction and joy). This kind of engagement is fundamentally generous on the part of the organization that cultivates it. If the engaged comes back to become a teacher or to endow a bunch of money after they discover a comet or the cure for something, that's great . . . but it's just happenstance. Successful leadership cultivates the soil; engagement is the fruit. Not the other way around.

> ### Successful leadership cultivates the soil; engagement is the fruit.

Unfortunately for my dog, I decided to pursue the HR angle a little further. Maybe this wasn't just management trying to squeeze extra blood from a tired stone. It was benefit-of-the-doubt time. With stalwart devotion to understanding my ideal, I dove in.

What Is Engagement?

To my relief, some scholars were forthright in their confusion. In many ways, the science of engagement is still trying to figure out how to define itself.

The most honest rendering of the question may be in *Evaluating the Evidence on Employee Engagement and Its Potential Benefits to NHS Staff: A Narrative Synthesis of the Literature.*[2] Chapter 3 of the report, frankly titled "What Is Engagement?," leans into the morass.

The authors immediately brought up a scholar whose name would show up again and again: "In his seminal article, Kahn claimed that personal engagement or disengagement arises when 'people bring in or leave out their personal selves during work-role performances.'"[3]

This is William A. Kahn, Everett W. Lord Distinguished Faculty Scholar at Boston University's Questrom School of Business. His research into why things go right and wrong in the workplace spans forty years. His takes on what makes for fertile ground mirror many of my own. When I read this prior sentence, I was hopeful. Then things went awry.

"However, along with this burgeoning interest has been considerable confusion and uncertainty about what engagement means, leading Christian et al.[4] to conclude: 'engagement research has been plagued by inconsistent construct definitions and operationalizations.'"

Ruh-roh.

Kahn continued, "The emerging consensus is that engagement is a psychological state . . . 'a relatively enduring state of mind referring to the simultaneous investment of personal energies in the experience or performance of work.'"

This left me a little cold again because it defined engagement by how it is applied, not by what it is. The report I mentioned above goes on to ponder whether an employer is seeing a "work task or job engagement" in an industrious employee, whether engagement is the product of an "employment relations practice," and whether engagement is "the opposite of burnout."

The whole thing left me disheartened. I had never felt such a disconnect between research and practice. But I'm nothing if not persistent, so I widened the search. A handful of frameworks began to surface. If you're the type who likes the deep dive, there's a sidebar that follows. If not—no judgment.

A FEW THEORIES OF ENGAGEMENT BY PEOPLE IN LAB COATS

The **study of "mindsets" and employee engagement** distinguishes between fixed and growth mindsets. The literature suggests that people with growth-oriented beliefs are more likely to embrace challenges and persist through tough times. It uses cognitive-behavioral principles to unlock potential and *unleash* engagement.[5] At a glance, this struck me as hot-rodding an employee, even altering their personality, to a designated end. Maybe that's an unkind reading. Maybe I missed the point.

Similarly, the **social psychology of engagement** examines how personality traits, such as extraversion and openness, influence engagement through social connections. It highlights the role of rewards—in this case, social rewards like recognition—in driving motivation.[6]

Both of these techniques included some elements I recognized...but they also felt a little extractive and did not remind me of the kind of engagement I identified with. Next!

Public sector engagement models come to the very reasonable conclusion that immediate supervisors impact employee engagement, with a premium on feedback, recognition, and opportunities for growth.[7] Again, the definition of *engagement* proves elusive, but the importance of feedback and recognition (being seen and heard) is undeniably common to my world.

Job Demands-Resources (JD-R) Theory proposes, almost mathematically, that engagement arises when job resources balance job demands. Burnout comes from excessive demands with inadequate resources. Engagement flourishes when resources attenuate stress.[8] Simple as that: Don't light the candle at both ends, and it won't burn out so fast. Engagement solved. Pass.

Research into interpersonal relationships and engagement in education shows how the connections between teachers and students—and among peers—can significantly influence motivation, curiosity, and a student's willingness to lean in. I couldn't help but think about some of our deliberate community-building practices at our Science at Sea and Science in the Rockies excursions (more to come on both later). A supportive community really does make all the difference in creating a safe environment for connection. Trust, empathy, and positive reinforcement help build emotional connections, which lead to better learning outcomes.[9] Check, check, and check.

The **study of engagement and psychological presence** by W. A. Kahn felt much more familiar. Kahn's theory (a classic in the field) emphasizes psychological presence, where employees or students feel valued, focused, and emotionally invested in their roles. It highlights meaningful work, role clarity, and authentic connections as drivers of engagement.[10] Again, I liked Kahn's thinking because it felt more like an explanation than an office hack.

Lastly, **Training Engagement Theory** examines engagement during skill acquisition and training, focusing on multilevel learning systems that combine cognitive, emotional, and behavioral strategies. I don't know if this is engagement as I know it—but I can't say it isn't, either. It's certainly fascinating stuff, and the value it places on active involvement is much more intuitive to an educator like me.[11]

E. N. Beattie's *The Power of Positive Leadership* draws from positive psychology and applied neuroscience to highlight how supportive leadership creates an environment of psychological safety that leads to intrinsic motivation. Now we're talking! Leaders who practice positive reinforcement and emotional intelligence indirectly encourage creativity and resilience in their reports. The theory suggests that the brain's reward systems respond positively to optimism and recognition, enhancing productivity and reducing stress.[12] I'll buy some of that stock.

To their credit, most of these scholars manage to identify some solid, basic requisites for engagement: Trust, belonging, and collaboration are encouraged in almost every case.

Some writers—such as Paul Zak[13]—posit that trust is the defining characteristic of a work culture that encourages engagement. I like this approach because it acknowledges that trust is a two-way street. The employee must trust their manager to do their best work, and that trust is earned by the employer trusting the employee to work as they see fit.

Admittedly, this brings up the most distinguishing factor between engagement in work and in education: In education, students are always moving on their own private track in parallel with their classmates. Teamwork must be arranged deliberately through projects and collective experiences. In the workforce, there's only one track, and everyone is on it together. Teamwork is implied.

Weirdly, most or all the prescriptive approaches I found seemed to ignore the possibility that an employee might influence an organization's trajectory rather than just its momentum. Most of what I read seemed bent on convincing or even tricking an employee into bringing their full self to bear on a predetermined task, but without room for the employee to determine what that task might be. At the most liberal end of the spectrum, an employee was granted the "freedom" to tackle a predetermined task as they saw fit.

For my money, I just don't think that allows enough space to fully engage.

Chemicals

There was, of course, a prevailing biological explanation for nearly every observable employee behavior. Unfortunately, this approach often leads inquiries (scholarly and popular) to a preoccupation with oxytocin and dopamine, which they place "at the heart of all desirable actions."[14] That sounded a lot like lab rats with a cocaine button to me, and frankly, it gave me the willies.

It's hard to make that kind of biological determinism jibe with what I see in the eyes of a child who has just discovered her passion for science. Even the tempting field of the neuroscience of learning sometimes (though not always) falls back on the dopamine reward system as the intrinsic motivating factor behind engagement and education.[15]

I love dopamine as much as the next hominid, but that approach to education, engagement, and love strikes me as intensely dehumanizing.

Your Engagement Belongs to You

The essential difference between the kind of engagement an employer prods from their employee and the kind of engagement I'm looking for is that, in my kind, the color and shape of the goal shift based on each person. That's because true engagement comes out looking like an individual, not like a job description. It belongs to them in an intimate way, and the surrounding apparatus (whether a lab, a classroom, a conference center, an art studio, or an office) shifts to accommodate the blooming individual, not vice versa. I have no interest in squaring a circle.

Dr. Holcombe, in her wisdom, completely understands this, and she expressed it better than I ever could:

> I have recently been very drawn to a framework for playful learning. Joyful learning is an aspect of that broader framework. In science, there's a misunderstanding that if your students are having fun, if it looks like play, then they must not be learning, which is not at all the case. The framework of playful learning has an aspect of joy. What does it mean to be joyful? How do we know joy is happening?
>
> When you put empowerment, meaningful learning, and joyful learning together, it becomes playful learning, but it also

becomes engagement. It is inherently engaging. It's community, it's problem-solving, it's the intrigue of asking a question that doesn't have an answer yet. It's the choice of being able to decide what it is you are going to try to figure out.[16]

Wow. I suggest you make some genius friends too. When Dr. Holcombe first shared her work on playful learning with me, I remembered an experience I had purposely tried to forget for the past twenty years.

In the mid-'90s, I met a wonderful chemistry professor by the name of Dr. Jim Giulianelli, who taught at Regis University in Denver, Colorado. "Dr. G" was well known for his summer science institutes for teachers, combined with a hands-on science camp for kids. I immediately fell in love with his unique approach to professional development for teachers. Instead of sitting in a lecture hall discussing best practices and instructional strategies for getting students excited about learning science, Dr. G crafted an experience in which teachers became the students and conducted the experiments and lessons for themselves instead of learning about them from a PowerPoint presentation. I watched as a room full of teachers rekindled their childlike enthusiasm for learning. It was playful learning in practice (which, I guess, is the only kind of playful learning).

In a partnership with Denver Public Schools, Dr. G invited 120 children between the ages of eight to twelve to attend a summer science camp. And who became those kids' personal science coach and all-around superhero? That's right, one of the teachers from the morning session. With a one-to-four teacher-student ratio, each teacher could put into practice the engagement strategies and best practices with their four new best friends. It was a total win-win. The summer camp became a formative assessment, allowing each teacher to observe, gather feedback, and adjust instruction in real time. It was a learning experience for both sides—refining instruction while learning took place. Magic.

I was honored when Dr. G invited me to serve as his codirector. His unique model of instruction caught the attention of the National Science Foundation and other granting agencies, and they funded our camps for nearly a decade. The weeks were filled with things that fizz, pop, and explode. *Ooohs* and *ahhhs* oozed from the labs in the Regis University Chemistry Department. It was truly a *best day ever* experience for this young science teacher.

We had just wrapped maybe the best few weeks of camps we had ever held. Everything seemed to click. One afternoon during the week of cleanup (there was a lot of cleanup), the department chair asked me to stop by her office. I thought she might want to reflect on the excitement of the camps and the possibility that these children might want to grow up to become scientists.

"Steve, I know you don't have a doctorate in chemistry or education, so I don't expect you to fully understand what I'm about to say," she said as I tensed in my seat. "I know that you and Dr. G are having fun as you play with the teachers and kids, but I would be doing myself a disservice if I didn't tell you how much I disagree with what you're doing."

I could feel the blood draining from my face.

"Do you see that certificate on the wall?" She pointed to her doctoral degree. "That degree represents the years of my life I put into the hard work and dedication needed to earn my credentials. I treat my job as a professor seriously. The field of organic chemistry should be taken seriously. But all I hear coming from the labs, the classrooms, even the hallways over the last few weeks is laughter and screwing around. The so-called teachers are teaching science tricks in labs where *real* learning takes place the rest of the academic school year."

I felt like I had been punched in the gut. I truly couldn't speak.

"My only hope is that one day these students will realize science isn't all fun and games—it's a serious business that requires hard work and years of dedication to their field of study. Honestly, the only reason I allow the camps to go on in my chemistry department is because of the NSF grant attached to Dr. Giulianelli's outreach work."

Silence.

I stood up, thanked her for sharing her thoughts, and closed the door behind me as I left. As I walked away, my only thought was, *How could someone so smart and accomplished fail to see the value in the seeds we planted in the lives of the children and educators who attended our camps?*

As I reflect on this today, I realize that the professor with the PhD in organic chemistry suffered from the misunderstanding that if learners, old and young alike, are laughing and having fun, if it looks like play, then they must not be learning. Unfortunately, she's not alone. In the many years that have followed, I have encountered dozens of like-minded administrators, executives, supervisors, and managers who are intolerant of *play* and *joy* in the workplace. I'm sure the same *this-is-serious-business* soliloquy has been uttered in countless boardrooms and offices by well-intentioned leaders who could benefit from the research of Dr. Holcombe and her colleagues in the science of engagement.

Loose Conclusions on a Young Field

I'm not a neuroscientist or a behavioral scientist or an HRD scholar, and I am *definitely not* saying that all the scholarly work mentioned here is hogwash. But my glimpse into the hard science of engagement showed me a field in its infancy, a field still defining its core terms (even its own name). It doesn't have as much to do with what I try to do as I had hoped it would, but there are glimmers of kinship.

The shadow of what I experience as a leader in the best of times is in there . . . but only as a shadow. While I acknowledge that the classroom and the boardroom are two different places, I can't embrace a vampiric definition of engagement, one that sees the unique power of the engaged individual as an asset to be exploited for the good of a business or organization. That said, I also don't believe those who pursue employee performance are doing anything wicked. I just think we're talking about two different things.

Engagement isn't about hacking motivation or squeezing more effort out of people. It's about creating environments where individuals feel valued, supported, and connected.

The big takeaway for me is this: Engagement isn't about hacking motivation or squeezing more effort out of people. It's about creating environments where individuals feel valued, supported, and connected. Whether in the workplace or the classroom, the most effective engagement strategies prioritize meaning, relationships, and psychological presence—not just external rewards or productivity metrics.

Apologies to those who might disagree, but playful learning is what engagement looks and feels like to me.

The Lesson

- Engagement isn't compliance; it's capacity. It's not about getting people to perform. It's about unlocking something in them they didn't know was there.
- Connection creates safety, and safety drives participation. When people feel seen and supported, they're more likely to take risks and stay present.
- Joy and curiosity are essential, not extra. Play isn't a break from learning; it's often the best way in.
- Trust is the prerequisite for growth. You can't mandate engagement. You earn it.
- Science is still catching up. The research matters, but the best practitioners already know how engagement feels—and how to build it.
- Engaged people aren't passive; they're partners. They help shape the moment. They cocreate the experience.

CHAPTER 10

"CUFF THE KID"

WHEN I WAS EIGHT YEARS OLD, I WALKED HOME FROM SCHOOL ONE frigid Wednesday afternoon to find the 9NEWS Action Cam parked in front of my house.

The 9NEWS Action Cam!

There were only three stations in my town at the time, and 9NEWS was *the* station.

They're either taking my dad to jail, or something cool is happening! I thought as I broke into a run and burst into the house to find Ward Lucas, news anchor extraordinaire, sitting in my living room.

Before I could get a word out of my mouth, Dad said, "Steven, go get your handcuffs."

"Yes, sir," I said with a little pep in my step.

Magic house. We all had handcuffs. I fetched mine.

"Steven, give those cuffs to Mr. Lucas."

I proffered my handcuffs to Ward Lucas, news anchor.

"Cuff the kid," Dad said.

Ward Lucas looked to his cameraman for help, then back at my dad. "I am not going to cuff the kid."

The two-man 9NEWS crew was there to learn about scams people were running in Denver. Carny types had been rolling through downtown doing the three-card monte and such, scamming people out of cash. The Denver Police Department (DPD) figured my dad would know a thing or two about that kind of ruse—which of course he did, more than they could ever imagine.

During the course of his consultation with the DPD, Dad had happened to say, "By the way, you guys should know that it's pretty easy to get out of your cuffs."

The police didn't buy it.

"Cuff the kid," Dad said to Ward Lucas.

"No."

"Just do it," my dad said with a funny smile only I would understand.

"These look like real cuffs."

"They're the same ones the Denver police use. Hands behind your back, Steven."

I put my hands behind my back, and Ward Lucas, news anchor, cuffed me on camera. He knew what he was doing. He even pushed in the deadlock on both wrists. On an eight-year-old!

When I went to fetch the handcuffs, I had hidden a bobby pin in the back pocket of my jeans. That's all you need to shim a cuff. While Dad and Ward Lucas were chatting, I swept the keyhole to release the deadlock pin and shimmed both cuffs in about thirty seconds.

"Steven," Dad said, "do you have anything to share with Mr. Lucas?"

"Here's the handcuffs," I said, cuffs dangling from my third-grade fingers.

Ward Lucas looked like he had seen a ghost.

"Why don't you show Mr. Lucas how you did that?"

It was one of the very first times I had ever been allowed to teach a secret.

"But he's not a magician," I said, making sure this wasn't a test.

"He's kind of like a magician," said Dad. "You can teach him."

So I showed Ward Lucas, news anchor, how to shim a pair of police-issued handcuffs.

For the next six months, Lucas paraded Denver police officers through my parents' magic school two or three at a time to take the escapes class. I'd walk in there, eight years old, and Lucas would say, "All right, Bob. Take your handcuffs and cuff the kid."

These Denver police officers would be looking for the door.

"I am not cuffing the kid."

"Seriously. You've got to cuff the kid."

Those were even easier, because police officers sit and ratchet their cuffs when they're bored. They ratchet them through over and over again, and that makes the spring loose. It was so easy to get out of those. The cops were gobsmacked.

"If this kid can get out of these using a bobby pin," my dad said, "there's a three-card monte dealer out there who can do it in the back of your car."

Some of those officers took magic classes for years afterward.

***

Ward Lucas passed away recently. I told this story to a small gathering of his friends and family at his funeral.

Could Dad have gotten out of the cuffs himself? In a heartbeat. Possibly underwater. But he needed shock and awe to get his point across. The magic was a very powerful tool, but it was the presentation that made it unforgettable.

You might never have the opportunity to perform an escape act for the 9NEWS Action Cam. That's rarefied air. But every experience you put together for your team (juvenile or adult) is an opportunity to push it a little further than they expect. Surprise makes a dramatic impression, and a dramatic impression has a way of inviting connection.

Surprise makes a dramatic impression, and a dramatic impression has a way of inviting connection.

The Lesson

- When people feel seen, they show up differently. Recognition opens the door to trust, and trust opens the door to engagement.
- Sometimes all it takes is a moment. A glance, a word, a gesture—that's often all someone needs to know they matter.
- You don't need a grand gesture to make a lasting impact. The small moments stick because they're real.
- Creating a connection isn't about performance; it's about presence. Be there. Pay attention. That's often enough.

CHAPTER 11

BE THE BAD BOY

S A BRAND-NEW TEACHER WITH A SHOWBIZ BACKGROUND, I BECAME obsessed with what earned and held the kids' attention. I didn't have kids yet, but I remembered being a kid. Pizza for lunch—does that get my attention? Maybe, if I'm young enough. Long division? Only if I've struggled in math or if long division is particularly valued at my house. What if there's a fire drill? No, probably not . . . but what about an *actual fire*? Bingo. A harmless electric shock? Yes, definitely.

It all came into focus. The kids engaged with the lessons when they were memorable and invited connection, involvement, and investment. And that almost always hinged—be it ever so slightly— on breaking some rules.

The flaming book was great for this, but so was a controlled explosion (more on that later) and slime. Lots of slime. Sometimes, you have to be the bad boy to get a little attention. Every sibling knows this intuitively. But by being a little bit of a deviant as a leader, you give permission to those who follow you to be as goofy as they want to be. You can make a lot of connections that way if you're brave enough to let them happen.

Kids want a teacher who has lost his or her mind.

Kids want a teacher who has lost his or her mind. They want somebody who takes it to the nth degree and then pushes it further. Somebody so passionate about what they do that they'll spend a crazy amount of time orchestrating a shared experience.

"I get it, Steve," you protest. "Erupting mountains of foam and electrified pickles and flying potatoes and all that. It's cute. But it isn't for adults."

That is where you are wrong, Dearest Reader.

The reason Elephant Toothpaste "works" with kids is that it demonstrates the chemistry I'm trying to teach them. You're probably not trying to teach chemistry to adults, but if you were (and I do, professionally), the exact same stuff would work exactly as well.

If the term "Elephant Toothpaste" is new to you, either scan the QR code or Google Elephant Toothpaste to see why kids love this reaction.

You remain unconvinced. No problem. I have a story that should convince you.

Automated Typesetting
vs. Free Cheesecake

An editor friend of mine attended the Association of University Presses's annual conference. Every conference features an opportunity for the publishing professionals to eat a free dessert while a medley of vendors present their publishing products one by one. It is so dull that most people buy their own dessert elsewhere, but my friend heard there would be cheesecake, so he attended.

One of the vendors was selling software that automated typesetting. Snore. The vendor was in his twenties. He wore rectangular photochromic glasses that darkened beneath the stage lights. He walked to the microphone and said, in an impossibly mirthless monotone, "Who has a copyedited manuscript they can send me?"

A few people looked up from their cheesecake. "Is he talking to us?"

"Seriously," said the vendor, deadpan. He clicked his laptop, and a slide appeared on the screen behind him. It was just an email address. "Somebody send me a finished book in a Word doc. First one in my inbox gets it typeset for free, right now."

Typesetting is expensive and time-consuming. A few people, mostly production folk like my friend, took out their phones and fiddled with them. In a few seconds the guy on stage said, robotically, "Joelle Phillips?" A woman at my friend's table raised her hand, wary. "Joelle, you are our lucky winner. You have submitted . . . *Ethnographies of Suspicion: Anthropologists as Subjects in Participant Spaces*. Watch the screen, please."

The email address vanished, and the dashboard of the automated typesetting software appeared. Then, a stopwatch timer popped up in the bottom right corner.

"I am starting the timer now," said the vendor.

The stopwatch began counting in seconds with milliseconds blazing by in a blur. *Ethnographies of Suspicion* appeared as a Word doc on the dashboard.

"The program is coding the manuscript based on predominant fonts and styles," said the vendor.

Twenty seconds passed. The Word doc blinked and skimmed on its own as hundreds of operations were executed. At thirty-three seconds, it stopped.

"Now that the manuscript is coded, the program can flow it into InDesign."

Forty-five seconds. The graphic design program called InDesign opened within the dashboard. A few book designers in the room perked up with recognition. *Ethnographies of Suspicion* flashed page by page into InDesign, already looking like a typeset book. It was three hundred and fifty-two pages long with three hundred footnotes.

The sound of attendees sitting their forks down pierced the growing silence. All eyes were on the screen now.

"We choose a template." He clicked a menu onscreen. Fifty-five seconds. "I like this one for anthropology. Joelle, do you prefer the main title or chapter titles for running heads?"

"Um."

"We're on the clock, Joelle."

The place roared with a collective laugh. Every slice of cheesecake was forgotten.

"Chapter titles, please," said Joelle.

"Footnotes or endnotes?"

"Endnotes, please."

One minute and thirty seconds. The vendor clicked three boxes and a button that said *SET*, and the program flew into a frenzy of pages. The stopwatch hummed away in the corner while page by page of *Ethnographies of Suspicion* flashed forward, then backward at apparent random. When the flashing was over, the clock read two minutes and twenty-five seconds.

"PDF OK, Joelle?"

"Super."

One more click and a rendering wheel appeared over the InDesign window. When the wheel stopped turning, the stopwatch froze at 3:48:15. Without a word, the presenter closed the dashboard window and double-clicked the only file in a folder he had ready: a PDF labeled *Ethnographies of Suspicion*. He opened it and scrolled through a beautifully typeset PDF.

"I'll email this to you, Joelle."

He closed his laptop and walked offstage.

"People lost their minds," my friend told me later. "It was like Adele had just finished her encore. The guy had a line at his booth for the rest of the weekend. I overheard designers plotting his assassination."

✳

I'm sure there are more boring products than automated typesetting software, but none come to mind. This guy captivated an entire room of professionals who came *ready to be bored*, and he did it by breaking a bouquet of rules:

- **He violated the sanctity of boredom.** People might be expecting you to be dull; some might even prefer it. Do not be cowed or bullied by low expectations.
- **He asked for things he shouldn't have.** By publicly exchanging email addresses with a stranger, he was committing a harmless but distinct social faux pas. By asking for a proprietary manuscript, he was inviting everyone in the room—especially Joelle—to become accessories to a breach in editorial etiquette.

- **He turned something professional into a game.** The stop-watch not only made the actual act of the work fun for three minutes and forty-eight seconds, but it also undermined the whole notion that it had to be unfun at all.
- **He committed to the character of the unassuming computer guy instead of pretending to be something he wasn't.** These kinds of panels are full of phony ringmasters, people pretending to have "big" personalities. It's like a parade of car dealership commercials. The computer guy tapped into a secret that will serve you for your entire leadership life: All personalities are big, even yours.

Bad boys get attention by surprising and by pushing boundaries. They scale up. They do a cool thing, and then they say, "But wait! What if we . . . ?!" They set you up for a surprise again and again and again.

> **Bad boys get attention by surprising and by pushing boundaries. They scale up.**

It feels good to do this. It feels clever. But you have to be several more steps ahead than they think you are. That's a technique we can all use, whether we're doing it with kids or with clients. Look three steps down the road and defy expectations.

"What if we did this? And this? And this?!"

You may find yourself in company so stiflingly prim that they are appalled by your lack of decorum. So be it.

If what you did was transformational, if you changed the way a person sees, feels, thinks, and reacts, even on a small scale, then you crafted an experience with an eye toward connection and engagement.

Our superpower as leaders is creating experiences that change lives. We rarely unlock that superpower without breaking a few rules.

> ## Our superpower as leaders is creating experiences that change lives.

The Lesson

- Disruption, when done with intention and heart, creates space for people to wake up and lean in.
- Joyful rule-breaking invites curiosity. It signals that something different is about to happen—and that's where engagement starts.
- Being the "bad boy" isn't about ego or chaos. It's about knowing your audience well enough to stretch the boundaries for their benefit, not yours.
- Sometimes the best connection comes after the unexpected. Surprise breaks routine—and people remember what breaks the routine.
- You don't have to be outrageous to be effective, but you do have to be willing to take a risk. Playing it safe rarely makes anyone feel something.

CHAPTER 12

SQUIDY: A SAGA

DAD MADE ME A SCIENCE TOY CALLED A CARTESIAN DIVER WHEN I was five years old. I guess he wanted to help me change things up a little. Sharing a science experiment for show-and-tell would be a nice change of pace.

Named after the eighteenth-century scientist and mathematician René Descartes, the Cartesian diver is a simple device. An eyedropper held a certain amount of water in it. I put it into a plastic soda bottle nearly full of water. The dropper floated because of the air trapped inside the bulb. But when I squeezed the bottle, even subtly, the air inside the bulb compressed, causing the water level in the eyedropper to go up. The little diver toy sank. When I released the squeeze, it floated back up to the top of the bottle. Sink and float, sink and float. Magic.

"Steven," Dad said. "Since this is a science experiment, we're going to practice explaining the science of how this works. It's called Boyle's Law—pay attention."

I know that's expecting a lot of a five-year-old, but that's my dad. "Yes, sir," I said.

But I had other ideas. I practiced squeezing the bottle in such a way that it was undetectable. I got good at it. I could make the dropper dance. With a secret squeeze, I could increase the pressure and cause the eyedropper to sink. Releasing my squeeze ever so slightly would decrease the pressure, and the silly little eyedropper would float. Then I brought it to school.

"Hey, what's in the bottle?" a friend asked. It was a little strange for a five-year-old to be carrying around something like this on the playground.

"This device will tell us if you have magical powers with your finger," I told the gathering crowd of kids. "Watch this . . . I have magic powers. I lightly touch the outside of the bottle with my finger to magically cause the eyedropper to obey my every command."

I pointed to the eyedropper and squeezed slightly as I led it downward with my magic finger.

"Randy, you try it."

Randy Cox put his finger where mine had been and tried to lead the diver downward. I didn't squeeze. The diver remained inert.

"Hmm. Doesn't seem to be working. I guess Randy has no magic powers. Who's next? It only costs a quarter to try."

Lunch cost fifty cents, so most kids had two quarters rattling around in their pocket. They gave me their quarters, and if I liked them, I squeezed the bottle to make the diver go up and down. They had magic powers. They could do it as much as they wanted to.

"Who's next? Who wants to try it?"

I was an up-and-coming carnival barker. Just like with the three-card monte trick, it was 99 percent about the presentation and 1 percent about the trick itself. Nobody ever asked me how it worked. Nobody said, "You're squeezing it." There were such powerful, personal stakes—a magical finger!—nobody could challenge it.

My friends were all twenty-five cents short at lunch because a kid dressed in a plaid shirt with nicely combed hair had scammed them on the playground. Everyone went home hungry but me. I came home with a few bucks jingling in my pocket, totally proud. I didn't see it as a scam at all. Just entertainment, right? You get paid to be an entertainer. I took the money to Dad and told him all about it.

"How did they buy lunch?" he asked.

"They didn't."

"Did you?"

"Yes, sir." Clouds started to darken my pride.

"You can't do that," he said. "You have to give the money back."

I had learned another valuable lesson about presentation and inviting others into the experience. I had also learned that these lessons could be abused, and that abusing them made me feel bad.

Right technique, wrong motivation.

$$*$$

Fast-forward to the mid-'90s. I had landed a side hustle conducting a weekly science experiment on a local kids' television show. (More on that later.) After all those years, I finally had my chance to do right by Boyle's Law. But, as it turns out, TV cameras can't detect a clear eyedropper very well. I set out to find a way to "decorate" it.

Walking the aisles of Walmart stimulates my creativity. After striking out in the toy department, I widened my circuit, and a glimmering object in the sporting goods section caught my eye. I don't fish, so I didn't know anything about the fisherman's endless variety of hooks and jigs and rubber worms, but the neurons and dendrites in my brain started to dance when I saw what looked to me like a shiny rubber squid.

By this time, the guy working the fishing section could sense my excitement.

"Can I answer any questions?" he asked.

"These squid-like things . . . are they hollow? Do you think they would fit over an eyedropper?" I said with far too much excitement in my voice.

"Not a clue," he said. "But you have your choice of salmon or trout flavor."

"Would you mind if I opened the package to see if the squid fits over this eyedropper?"

"You open it . . . you buy it."

The good news was that Renée had slipped twenty dollars in my pocket for my little Sunday outing. This gave me just enough capital for some serious research and development. I gathered up my smelly rubber squids ($18.35 worth, to be exact) and headed home.

The kitchen quickly became my laboratory as I searched for a way to fit the rubber squids over the eyedropper. Amazing discovery: If you put a rubber squid in the microwave for exactly seven seconds, the rubber softens up just enough to make it easy. When Renée recounts the story, she points out that the smell of trout-infused rubber never quite left the microwave. But the darn thing worked! While my television producer appreciated my solution, my elementary students *loved* the new water toy, aptly named SQUIDY. By the end of the school day, every kid owned a new pet squid that could sink and float on command. The microwave in the teacher's lounge forever smelled like fish and mildly burnt rubber after that.

Renée is a really smart cookie. She sees things differently than I do and solves problems with a different level of thinking. That's why it should come as no surprise that she suggested I reach out to the fishing lure manufacturer to see if they could a) make a squid that could fit over the eyedropper without having to microwave it and b) remove that trout smell.

Much to my surprise, someone at the manufacturing company in Pasco, Washington, took pity on this science teacher and listened to my pitch.

"Yep, we can make a custom order of squid lures, item #BA-623. But I have to tell you right now that this lure will never catch a fish," said a nice man who knew he was dealing with someone who was a few clowns short of a circus.

"What might this cost?" I asked with trepidation in my voice.

"The mold will cost five hundred dollars, and each squid will cost twenty-five cents. You just need to fulfill the minimum quantity."

I was fairly certain Renée would give me the green light, so I placed the order while I had the helpful man on the phone.

"No problem," I said.

I sent over the necessary "company" information (we whipped up a name that—little did we know—would dominate decades of our lives: *Steve Spangler Science*) and wrote a check for the $500 that was due up front.

Three weeks later, a Yellow Freight truck pulled into my driveway late in the afternoon. The driver told Renée that he had a delivery from a company in Washington. My little science project had arrived.

The driver proceeded to unload three pallets of boxes wrapped in plastic.

"What's this?" Renée demanded.

"Beats the heck out of me," the driver said. "Sign here and I'm on my way."

Renée was standing in front of the pallets when I pulled into the driveway. She wore *that look*—a look I had come to know all too well.

"Your squids are here," she said in a tone I had never heard before.

That's right, the nice salesman at the fishing lure company in Pasco, Washington, he who had taken my order for the "minimum quantity," had sent out exactly that minimum number—*eighty thousand* custom-sized, black and neon pink, squid-like fishing lures, minus the trout scent, to the world headquarters of Steve Spangler Science.

There was paperwork attached to the front of one of the pallets. Renée and I opened the invoice together. Amount due: $20,000 (that's 80,000 x 25¢)—plus shipping.

Renée started to cry. As we comforted each other in the middle of our driveway, I couldn't help but think . . . *I wonder if the squids will work*. Many years later, a therapist would tell me that I have a problem with timing, but that's a story for another day.

Where had I gone wrong? I'd forgotten to ask an essential question: What does the term *minimum quantity* mean? Renée and I were newly married. We didn't have an extra $200, let alone $20,000 . . . but our parents did. We remain grateful for the loan.

The good news is that the custom lure fit perfectly over an eyedropper and performed better than any Cartesian diver I had ever made. SQUIDY™ became the first official product in the Steve Spangler Science catalog. Let's just say I became highly motivated to sell those acrobatic squids. It's funny how desperation can turn into the mother of creativity.

I found new ways to perform the trick (I mean, "teach Boyle's Law"). We sold it at every teacher conference we could find. I came up with presentation techniques that involved plucking a hair from a spectator's head (OK, I didn't *really* pull out a hair) and pretending to lasso SQUIDY to pull him down to the bottom of the bottle. Fooled everyone. The teachers at the exhibit booth would always smile. Then they bought one.

Renée and I quickly learned how to use the desktop publishing software that came with our Macintosh computer. We wrote instructions, crafted marketing copy, and took a crash course in product packaging, all in an effort to repay that loan from our parents.

Same old story: a little magic, a little science, a little story, and make it about them.

This experience engaged my attention (by the collar) and changed my outlook on business forever. Truth be told, Steve Spangler Science never would have become an official company if not for that itty-bitty, tiny, super small, minimum quantity communication mistake. SQUIDY became a popular product in the educational toy genre. We paid back the loan (with a little interest for good measure) and used the proceeds to hire more employees and embark upon more SQUIDY-like adventures.

I demonstrated SQUIDY thousands of times in those early years. "If you like that, there's ten more items in our science kit to teach you how to *be amazing*. Your students will know Boyle's Law for life."

We founded Be Amazing Toys™ in the early 2000s. Renée served as the CEO and chief wrangler of forty-seven Denver-based employees, plus two overseas factories producing our line of hands-on science kits. She landed national accounts such as Target, the old Toys "R" Us, Walmart, Hobby Lobby, Disney, Oriental Trading, Lakeshore Learning, Bed Bath & Beyond . . . dozens and dozens of national retailers and catalog companies. When the Internet became the new marketplace, Be Amazing Toys enjoyed a nice place in the educational toy space.

What started as a clever way to teach Boyle's Law turned into a magic finger scam (let's just call it an engaging demonstration) and then the foundation of two of our businesses.

※

The SQUIDY saga is really about the power of presentation. I figured out how to sell my Cartesian diver by changing the way I presented it—turns out, engagement lives in the delivery. But SQUIDY taught me more than one lesson. When I was a kid, I "sold" the magic by making people feel like something special had just happened. That same instinct worked later in the classroom—and again when I became a squid peddler. The big takeaway? When you help people feel amazing, it has a funny way of coming back to you.

The Lesson

- Every innovative idea starts with uncertainty. It's easy to underestimate what looks like a silly side project until it becomes the spark for something bigger.
- You don't need a million-dollar lab or perfect timing to innovate. You just need the willingness to say yes to the unexpected.
- Mistakes in business aren't dead ends; they're doorways. Misjudging demand or overordering a product like SQUIDY might feel like a failure, but it often becomes the start of your real education.
- Engagement in entrepreneurship happens when your curiosity collides with someone else's need. That's where the magic starts.
- Creating products is one thing; creating a community around them is another. That requires trust, connection, and a sense of play.

CHAPTER 13

MASTER CLASS: SCIENCE AT SEA

VERY FEW YEARS, WE FLOAT A HUNDRED SCIENCE TEACHERS OUT into the Pacific Ocean. Only the hardiest survive.

OK, they all survive. But we do hope they return transformed. It should be clear by now that "experience creation" is scalable—from a flaming wallet for a hotel desk clerk to a cruise ship full of educators and their plus-ones. We apply everything we've learned when we load up the teachers and set sail for Alaska in what we call Science at Sea. It is our master class in creating an experience designed for connection and transformative engagement.

The Show Starts Before the Show Starts

Carly Reed is the nervous system of our operation. Some call her the "keeper of Steve." I have no problem with this. When I say *we* in everything that follows, I am talking about myself and Renée, but I'm also big-time talking about Carly.

Carly has worked with us for twenty years, and she sets some very high standards for us as an enterprise and for me as a speaker.

Someone recently asked her what it was like working with me for so long, and she said:

> I couldn't represent somebody if I didn't believe they were the same person offstage as they are onstage. Whenever Steve hangs out after a keynote, the lines take forever because he actually talks to people. Unlike a number of speakers and celebrities I've worked with in the past, Steve is adamant about sticking around until he sees everyone in the line. That's just who he is.
>
> Once, in a line like that, a lady called me over. She was about seven people back. She'd maybe been waiting fifteen minutes at this point. She said, "I've got to ask you a question, and please tell me the truth: Is he really the guy that he is onstage? I don't want it to be ruined when I get up there. One time, I got in the line to meet somebody, and it ruined everything. And I had rather just not know if it's that way."

Carly never told me what she said to that woman, but I'm 80 to 85 percent sure it was positive. That lady experienced something during the keynote, and she was willing to stand in line to connect at a deeper level. But she had been burned before, and she didn't want that experience ruined if the connection was going to go bad. One of Carly's superpowers is making sure we don't disappoint. And her powers are at their zenith during Science at Sea.

We book a big block of rooms on a Holland America cruise ship. Many people think they're just going on a science cruise. They are, but if they come ready, they're also going to experience a consciousness shift. A big part of that is getting to know them ahead of time.

Registration opens over a year in advance. The moment folks start registering, Carly is on the phone. She explains:

If you registered tomorrow, I'd call you just to talk. I talk to them many, many times to really learn why they're coming. A lot of people open up just through organic conversation. I don't have a list of questions I ask. I just talk to them. "Hey, I see you registered. I'm here if you have any questions." We start that connection from the beginning, so they feel connected and looked out for before they even get on their flight.

Our goal is the opposite of a phone tree. Phone trees are the worst. Neither Steve nor I has the patience for following a labyrinth of numerals to reach someone after we've already dialed a number. If we did that ("For Carly Reed, dial 2, then hit the pound key"), the experience would be over before it started. No connection. The last thing we want is for people to start regretting the trip before it even begins.

Before they even get there, I have a pretty good idea of who they are, and they have a good idea of who I am. I've set the stage with the expectation that if you call me, I'll call you back; if you write me an email, I'll write you back. It's simple, but not everybody does that. I send emails that are caring, not just logistical. By the time they get there, they're often pretty nervous. Surprisingly, going on a cruise to Alaska is scary for a lot of people. I'm here to ease their fears and help focus their energy on the unforgettable experiences that are right around the corner.

When I first started working for Steve, he impressed upon me the idea of how time can make or break an experience. Here's a simple example: When someone calls our office, a real person (usually me) answers the phone. If you buy into Malcom Gladwell's assertion that people form an opinion of you, your organization, classroom, dinner party, anything, after just sixty seconds, you understand why I put such value on time. I try to answer the phone on the first or second ring because it's unexpected in today's world, and the person on the other end of the conversation gets to connect with a real human being. Building a meaningful connection during our first interaction plays a huge factor in their decision to join us on our Science at Sea adventure.

On-Ramp

The trip kicks off in Vancouver, British Columbia, so we're off to a pretty compelling start—Vancouver is one of the most beautiful cities in the world. Go there. We lodge everyone in the famous Pan Pacific Hotel the night before we board. The views are breathtaking. Welcome materials await them on their beds.

At seven in the morning on day one, teachers from all over the country, sometimes from different parts of the world, walk into the dining room for what they expect will be a standard-issue confer-ence breakfast: a stale bagel and mediocre coffee, because that's what teachers typically get.

The dining room of the Pan Pacific looks out over the bay, and our ship is already there, waiting for us. Our people find their own laminated personal name tags awaiting them at assigned tables. They don't write their own name on a sticker. They don't eat alone. Their name is *known* already. Everything is personalized, and everything is taken care of.

Carly is usually the first person they see at the registration table. Unlike the typical "pick up your badge and tote bag" routine, this registration experience is different. Everyone hugs Carly and shares their experience getting to the hotel. I've seen participants burst into tears of gratitude when they meet Carly because of the connection

MASTER CLASS: SCIENCE AT SEA

they've already made with her. She cares, and they know it. Some even ask her to take a selfie with them. Genuine connection.

There's a beautiful breakfast buffet waiting for them. The seating is open. We encourage them to meet new friends by answering one basic question: "What experiences brought you to sitting with me at breakfast today?"

Immediately, the experience is changed. Their environment has shifted around them because they're being cared for, acknowledged with some forethought, and treated like we're glad they're there. (We are.)

✳

Let's pause for a moment and identify some skills we've already put into practice:

- We have prepared.
- We are many steps ahead.
- We (hopefully) surpassed their initial expectations.
- We have made it about them.

I'll let Carly describe what happens that first morning:

There's a lot happening in that moment at breakfast. We have people who have never traveled before. We have people who have never been outside the US. We have people who have never been on a ship. We've got a lot of emotions happening.

There are two things we're trying to do at this breakfast: First, we're trying to ground the group energetically to calm them and make them feel safe and cared for. They need to feel safe to go on this journey. Second, we're trying to sync them with one another and with Steve so that they can connect in the experience. A lot of that happens at this first touch. This is all before they even set foot on the ship, even though it's right there, just out the window, where they can see it. That is deliberate.

While we advertise this as a cruise for teachers, many of them bring their plus-one, who could be a spouse, a family member, or a good friend. The plus-one adds a new dimension to the experience. A room full of like-minded teachers is very different than a fifty-fifty split of teacher and nonteacher participants.

Typically, the teacher participants have spent some limited time with Steve at a full-day workshop, a summer institute, or maybe just as an audience member at a keynote presentation. The plus-one, on the other hand, has only heard about Steve and what he does. In all honesty, many of them are a little apprehensive about the next seven days at sea with a science guy.

Our goal is to use our first few hours together to create the opportunity for them to connect and engage with Steve and our team of naturalists. We want them to have an unexpected, transformational experience before they ever set foot on the actual cruise ship.

After everyone enjoys a wonderful breakfast, they're invited into the main meeting room. Before the program even starts, we hope they're excited because they feel seen, valued, safe, and full, which means they can allow themselves to have fun and connect.

That's when Carly gives me the thumbs-up, and I jump on stage to officially kick off the program. All the teachers, all the spouses, the plus-ones, our whole team—everybody's there. My task for the opening program is to prime everyone for engagement. I do that by showing them that we feel lucky to be with them, that we are as excited as they are, and that they are safe to engage. You can't engage *en garde*. Carly calls it the most important hour of the entire trip because it's when meaningful connections start to form, and each person begins feeling safe to engage at their own pace.

Everything has been designed to create an environment that allows for wonder, discovery, and exploration. We're setting them up so that we can let them go.

There's no exact formula to it. Carly doesn't say, "They're going to engage right *here*." Rather, we create an experience framed with significance so they can come into that engagement on their own. They're all totally different, but we've set the table in a way that is meant to build capacity in all of them, to inspire without pushing.

When my opening presentation is over, then comes the proof in the pudding. Our naturalist, John Scheerens, officially welcomes everyone to his home ... Alaska, the eighth wonder of the world. John is more than just a naturalist; he's a world-class teacher who loves to help people explore Alaska. Everyone in the room immediately falls in love with John.

So it's the morning of day one. They're in love with Carly, they're in love with John, and hopefully they like me enough not to jump overboard. Now we can board the ship.

They check into their cabins, and their luggage is delivered to them. It's high noon, and the ship sets sail at 4:00 p.m. Our guests roam around the ship on their own, still supercharged from the morning. At dinner that night, we sit together in our reserved section of the dining room. It is surrounded by windows, giving us breathtaking views on all sides. Everyone is pre-assigned a table to avoid that uncomfortable scramble to get a seat. Carly has a sixth sense when it comes to seating people together who have a good chance of making a meaningful connection. An energy exudes from our seating area. The laughter is contagious. Our team has learned to eat quickly in order to make our rounds to all the tables. And yes, an occasional card trick might accidentally fall out of my pocket. It's just in my DNA.

At this point, relationships—even real friendships—are already starting to congeal. This first day solidifies their ability to let go because of the sequencing of what happened that morning before they got on the ship.

Now, back to Carly:

I'm running around behind the scenes, meeting with the ship's staff, and making sure Steve and John have everything they need—but I never want people to see that. I don't want them to "see the cords," as we say.

Many years ago, Steve was booked to speak at a Disney property in Florida. He needed electricity on stage to power some gizmo, so he stretched the orange extension cord he travels with from his onstage table to an outlet on one side of the stage. We finished the A/V check and left to grab a cup of coffee. When we returned to the room, someone from the hotel was on stage fiddling with Steve's props.

"Excuse me, can I help you?" I said, running up the stage stairs.

"I'm just fixing the cords," said the gentleman, who was wearing an official hotel uniform.

"Steve needs electricity on stage," I said.

"If Steve needs power, it's my job to make it magically appear. Disney is a place where magic happens. There's nothing magical about an orange extension cord. My job is to make sure our guests never see the cords."

There's nothing magical about an orange extension cord.

It was a powerful lesson in creating experiences. The reward isn't in the applause or the recognition for how hard we worked behind the scenes. The joy comes when the moment unfolds so smoothly that no one even notices the work—it just *feels right*. That kind of magic doesn't happen by accident. I'll never forget learning that from a hotel A/V guy who understood what real showmanship looks like.

When our participants arrive at dinner, they're seated at a table with their travel companion and a group of new friends who surprisingly share similar interests. They've become instant friends. When we take away the friction of chaos, it allows people to let go much more easily. When people see friction and chaos, their safety net goes up.

One thing people have said over and over about the trip is, "I could just relax. If you told me to be somewhere at 8:00 a.m., I would just be there, and everything would be taken care of." They sink into that, which takes away the guesswork. We remove all those things so they can just . . . be. Our goal is to create an environment in which they can level up. We put the spotlight on them and keep the responsibility on us. That's leadership.

Let's start a new list to see if we've followed our own advice to this point:
- Carly has been the maestro from the minute they registered, but her efforts have quadrupled now that everyone is together. The spotlight is on them, but the responsibility is on us.
- In the context of a weeklong trip, we definitely make the first touch count.

- Sequencing—from personalized name tags to an unexpected breakfast experience to the opening session with John and me—is deliberate.
- We (Team Spangler) are right there with them. Nobody is sequestered behind a curtain or at the captain's table.

Aboard

The first real day is a "full day at sea," as they call it in the cruising world. For the ship's passengers who are *not* part of our Science at Sea group, it's a day of bingo, shopping for diamonds, shuffleboard, and lots of drinking. We have something a bit different in store for our participants. Following breakfast, the Science at Sea'ers head to a private room to start their formal exploration.

On this particular venture, Carly and I debated what should happen next. My vote was to reintroduce our head naturalist, John, and let him kick things off with his opening lecture. Carly had a different idea. She thought I should take the first fifteen to twenty minutes and do a little magic—literally. A few tricks to get people laughing and ready to learn. *Think of it as an appetizer for the brain.*

The first year of the program, we did it my way, and it worked. But the second year, we tried Carly's approach—and there was a night-and-day difference. Did our naturalist need a warm-up act, like an emcee at a comedy club? No. He didn't need it. *But the audience did.*

One of Carly's superpowers is tuning into what people want and need before *they* even know it. In order for people to feel like they're in a safe zone and ready to learn, we need to remove apprehension and reassure them that everything is going to be OK.

When we first set out to create this trip, it was completely designed for teachers. But most of the teachers said, "Hey, I want to bring my spouse," or, "I want to bring my mother." It became a fifty-fifty split between educators and layfolk. That's unique in the big experiences we create, but Alaska fills the gaps.

We hold lectures on board about the natural wonders of Alaska, and then we take excursions to see them in person. We talk about whales, and then we go see whales; we talk about the glaciers, and then we go to the glaciers. Now they can more deeply connect with the experience because of the things John already told them in the comfort of the ship. It's different than if he were trying to yell facts as the whales were breaching. That's all part of the sequencing. We have to talk about whales before you go see them. It adds deeper meaning to what they're doing because it builds capacity in them that they then bring on the excursions.

When we get to Juneau, we've arranged whale-watching excursions. That's a nine-hour thing. The next day, we go to Skagway, which is a train trip. Two days later, we take them on a rainforest hike in Ketchikan.

One lady told me the biggest moment for her was seeing a banana slug in the rainforest. I never ever saw that coming. By the way, if you lick the banana slug, your tongue will go numb for a few hours. We both talked funny for the rest of the afternoon. At the end of the trip, she gave me a present—a refrigerator magnet of a banana slug with the saying, "If you love it, lick it." That magnet has a permanent home on my refrigerator.

I don't want to predict what their moments are. I want them to have those on their own. Some people cry when they see a glacier. They come to Carly with tears in their eyes, just from seeing something that resonated with them. It's Van Gogh.

Cultivate Wonder

We do everything possible to create an environment where new friends feel allowed to wonder. Ideally, you create this environment, and something happens on its own, but the excursions and the lectures are all about putting these teachers on solid ground where anything is possible. The goal is never to schedule them so hard that they have no time to stare at the ocean or play in the casino. What they need to do is more important than what we have planned for them. A big part of their experience is when they're not with us—the wonders they explore on their own.

An old friend of mine, Dr. Todd Wilcox, who was the best man at my wedding, called me one day and told me he wanted to come to Science at Sea. Todd's an orthopedic surgeon. Supersmart guy. Married. He came with his husband and two kids. I was honored to have Todd and his family on the trip, but truth be told, I was a little nervous. Todd is a really good friend, and I wanted everything to be perfect for him . . . if not perfect, at least great.

When we go on these excursions, one of our team leads says, "Hey, we're leaving at eight. If you're here, great. If you're not, you're on your own adventure!"

On the second or third day of our trip, the bus took off for wherever we were headed, and out the bus window, I saw Todd and his family walking down the street.

"Oh no, I lost Todd! Stop the bus!"

We stopped the bus in traffic. All these tourists were outside from the other cruises.

"Todd, I'm so sorry we left without you. Jump on."

Todd said, "No, no. Thanks, Steve. We're just going over here."

Ninety-six other people were on our buses. Todd and his family were the only ones not with us. But they had no intention of getting on the bus. He and his kids wanted to play on the playground and explore Skagway, Alaska, on their own terms. He loved it.

It was a learning moment for me, and I must admit that I didn't get it. We had planned a really cool excursion, and my best friend from school wasn't interested. But sometimes, I have to get out of my own head and alter my perspective. Todd and his family were enjoying *their* experience, not mine. Remember, the art of creating experiences is to leave room for others to connect and engage in their own way. The Engagement Effect is whatever it is. Once you've set the stage, it's time to relinquish control.

There are little details that are always fun to watch unfold. When it comes time to check out the whales on Auke Bay, everyone is quick to find their perfect whale-watching spot on the open deck. Inevitably, a few people notice a stranger with a really nice camera snapping photos of the scenery.

"Who's the new guy?" someone asks.

"Oh, that guy? This is *National Geographic* photographer Mark Kelley. He lives down the road from John Scheerens, and John suggested he come along to show you a few things about photographing whales. There's a copy of his award-winning book waiting for you in your room, by the way. And if you ask nicely, I'll bet he might just sign it."

Even people who don't dig photography are freaking out a little. Shock and awe. We could have announced it ahead of time. We could have put it in the brochure: Mark Kelley from *National Geographic*. But why would we do that? It would only pad the impact.

If you allow the discovery to be its own experience, people connect levels and levels beyond what they would if you made the experience into an agenda. When people figure it out on their own, they engage, whether they're five or fifty.

> If you allow the discovery to be its own experience, people connect levels and levels beyond what they would if you made the experience into an agenda. When people figure it out on their own, they engage, whether they're five or fifty.

The Carly Factor

Back to Carly for a moment. I would love to tell you that I taught Carly all these techniques, but we've learned them together over many, many created experiences. Carly has the ability to know how people should be connected to one another. Call it intuition, call it a special gift, but she knows when you and someone specific should be at a table together, and she makes that happen. Again, magic.

A lot of the people in those groups have now traveled to other events together. They didn't know each other before, and now they're great friends. They've gone on their own trips, and they've come back to ours. They've made lifelong friendships, and a lot of that starts that first morning at breakfast.

Every trip—*every* trip—some pair of people come to us with a new friendship and say, "How did you know?"

Carly connects with them on the phone in a way that the rest of us don't understand. By the time they're on the ship, Carly has already set the stage for them, individually, like the best teacher imaginable. Then, again like a great teacher, she leaves them alone. She explains:

> Once people feel safe, you just have to let them breathe. I don't want to tell them, "Look to your left." I want to put them in environments where they feel safe to open up, because that space is where they have these huge moments of engagement. It's never something I did directly; I just created the environment

that made it possible. That's when the real shift happens—when the experience deepens. I don't know how to explain that exactly except to say that you build capacity. Leadership is building capacity in another person and letting them go. If I say, "They're going to do this, this, this, this, and this, and then they're going to have these moments of connection and engagement," I've screwed up. If you substitute the word *engagement* with *care*, you see that they can all care about the same thing very differently, simultaneously.

Closing Session

On the last day at sea, we're headed back to Vancouver. John finishes up a few lectures, mostly details about Alaska that he still hasn't shared. The future of Alaska and the ecology and Arctic warming and that kind of stuff. A lot of people are very curious about that, which spurs a lot of discussion. To John's credit, he's more nervous about the last day—specifically his last lecture—than any of his other program responsibilities.

"I'm worried about the whole global warming thing," John says over a bourbon in a quiet corner of the ship. "In less than five minutes, I can alienate half of the group just by talking about the changes I've seen to the glaciers while living here. But I don't feel like I'm being honest and true to you or myself unless I give them a chance to ask questions and share their thoughts."

John hit the nail on the head. While I'm humbled that he would spend time worrying about offending one of our "clients" (John's words) and the financial impact it might have on future experiences, I'm so proud that he, too, gets it. He's not giving a lecture about the effects of climate change in Alaska; he's creating a space for highly engaged people to engage and connect at a new level, framed by a genuine sense of respect and authenticity.

Our final session with John would never be as powerful and impactful as it is without all the purposeful engagement strategies that have been woven into the fabric of the Science at Sea experience to that point. In all the years we've offered this trip, never once has anyone been offended by John's final observations about the changes he's personally witnessed or the scientific data he uses to help explain what's happening. On the contrary, participants can't wait to ask questions and share their thoughts and ideas.

During our 2024 trip, I was especially moved to watch how John facilitated conversation while answering some very pointed, personal questions. Our youngest participants shared their fears, and our more seasoned people offered thoughtful responses and even an apology or two for "screwing things up" for the next generation. Some moments were funny, and others provoked silence while people took a few seconds to think before responding.

John has a great sense of timing; he knows when it's time to wrap it up. As he shared his closing thoughts and gratitude for being part of the trip, I was struck by the fact that he had engaged us all for more than an hour without the mention of conservative or liberal ideology and without blame being thrust upon certain groups of people. He navigated the treacherous waters with the skill of a seasoned captain who finds joy in exploring the uncharted. We laughed, we cried, we hugged, and we stood on our feet and clapped as we shared our appreciation and respect for John's wisdom. I couldn't help but think of one of my favorite quotes from Dr. Nido Qubein, president of High Point University: "If all you have is information, people will use you and discard you. If all you have is knowledge, people will only call upon you when they need you. But if you have wisdom, they will always respect you."[17]

John's cup is overflowing with wisdom.

So, what's the lesson? When you're leading a conversation—whether it's in a classroom, a boardroom, or on a ship in the middle of the Inside Passage—what you say matters far less than how you say it. John reminds us that true engagement isn't about avoiding hard topics, but about creating a space where people feel safe enough to lean in, ask questions, and wrestle with the complexity. That kind of environment takes trust, timing, and a genuine respect for different perspectives. Be the guide who facilitates discovery, not the expert who dominates the dialogue. Engagement is built not on being right, but on being real.

Engagement is built not on being right, but on being real.

First Voice, Last Voice

I was the first voice they heard after breakfast at the Pan Pacific, and I'm the last voice they hear before they go to their last dinner together. Let's just say John's final session is a hard act to follow. The smart speaker would just close with the quote from Dr. Qubein and say goodnight. But that's the easy way out. I need to find a way to tie a bow on what we've experienced together before sending everyone on their way. I do something different every time based on the character of the group, but I always leave us on a high note.

At least, I try to. I'm working with a tough audience. Many times, they're really sad. By the time the last day rolls around, most of them are saying they don't want to go home yet, which is a wonderful problem. Check off another lesson: Keep it tight. Take your bow while they can still stand another trick. Don't be the poor sports guy who had to follow Immaculée Ilibagiza. Let them be in their emotions.

With those emotions in mind, I try to acknowledge their experience and just talk. At the very end, in our closing session, we all get together.

"I'm going to ask you a question. I ask kids this question as well. What was your *best day ever* moment from the last hour, the last day, the last seven days? What are the things that you'll never forget for the rest of your life? I know it seems like I'm implying that we created a life event for you. We didn't. *You* did."

As we go around the room, we get a hundred different answers. Not everybody says, "I liked the glacier." The answers are richer and specific to each individual because this experience has been *about them*, not me. We go all the way around the room. A hundred people. It takes forever, but it's worth it, and people are respectful of one another because that's the atmosphere we've cultivated. Once you open the box, you have to make time. If they feel comfortable enough to really share, your experience has inspired a connection. Magic.

A good leader makes people feel safe enough to connect at a higher, deeper level. That doesn't mean catering to their every need, but it does mean freeing them from some of the tedium that holds back their growth. But be ye warned: When they start growing in safety, they're going to connect with their authentic selves. You have to give them space, and you have to give them time to connect.

The Lesson

- Real engagement deepens when people leave their comfort zone and immerse themselves in a new environment.
- When the surroundings change, the learning changes. A ship in the Inside Passage becomes a floating classroom unlike any other.
- The best learning moments often aren't scheduled—they arise from curiosity, conversation, and shared observation.
- Letting people experience science, not just hear about it, builds lasting understanding and excitement.
- Sometimes the best facilitation strategy is to create the space and then step back so others can step up.

CHAPTER 14

VAN GOGH DOESN'T META

S O FAR, WE'VE TALKED ABOUT THE NUTS AND BOLTS OF SHOWMAN-ship, creating an experience, getting folks on board (sometimes literally), and having our ducks in a row. Specifically, we have learned that:

1. **Experience creation is about control.** Negative. Experience creation is about *connection*.

2. **You will create the same experience for everyone.** You won't. You can't. The closer you get to creating an identical experience for all, the more lifeless and limp that experience will become. Everyone enjoys food in their own way; everyone gets poisoned the same. Every kid reacts differently to every lesson. Any teacher will tell you that. The good ones will tell you that's the best part of teaching.

3. **Your experience is only as valuable as the outcome you plan.** Wrong, wrong, wrong. When you free an experience from a predetermined outcome, it becomes more powerful. Why? Because you send it back to the people you're leading and let them create the outcome naturally. They are all different, and they will infuse that difference into every experience, enriching

it, upgrading it, intensifying it. But only if *you* get out of the way.

That last part may be a sticking point for you.

"Never!" you say. "The moment I 'get out of the way,' everything will fall apart!"

Don't panic. I know the *letting go* part can be terrifying, especially for the control freaks among us. But relax; you're still the leader. The architect. You have created the experience. If you've done it right, if you've framed that experience well, connection and engagement are waiting at the threshold. But you have to stand back if you want them to squeeze through the door.

Hey, look! I have a story. . .

Meta, the Verb

I once spoke at the New England Mail Order Marketing Association. It was more fun than it sounds. The speaker before me gave a workshop about how *to meta*. A verb. One *metas* by identifying how a client acts, how they move, and how they talk, and then *meta*-ing those traits back at them.

"If you want someone to buy from you, just meta them," said the speaker. "If they're chill, you're chill. If they're hyper, you're hyper. Whatever it is, that's how you're going to sell your product. Once they see themselves in you, they're going to make decisions based on that."

To me, this sales approach felt like pure manipulation. The term "just meta them" seemed like a way of getting a potential buyer to feel like they were buying something from a friend. But friends don't use "sales techniques" on friends. Friends don't manipulate friends. This really got me to thinking about the importance of authenticity and the difference between *experience* and *manipulation*.

I had a very specific, somewhat unusual upbringing, as you've already seen. That upbringing, combined with my own personality, makes it easy for me to connect with a large audience. It's a gift I was given and have cultivated. If I didn't have that fortunate combination of traits and circumstances, would I feel inclined to *meta* instead? Was I being judgy? I really thought about it.

The person who set me straight was Vincent van Gogh.

Van Gogh, the Opposite

When our kids were growing up, our family got to vacation wherever I had a speaking gig. We went to Muscatine, Iowa; Plaster City, California; and every town in western Kansas.

But one year, when our boys were in elementary school, I landed a speaking engagement in Philadelphia. Holy moly—an actual big city! Renée plans everything to a T, so she sat down with the kids ahead of time.

"Boys, we're going to Philadelphia. What do you want to do?"

Scotty, age seven, said, out of the clear blue, "We should go see Vincent van Gogh's *Sunflowers* at the Philadelphia Museum of Art."

Renée and I looked at each other, wondering when aliens had absconded with our son and replaced him with this kid.

"Scotty, how do you know about that?"

"It was on *Baby Einstein*."

Fair enough. We were *those* parents. We let our young children watch visually stimulating videos that introduced them to basic concepts such as colors, numbers, classical music, and, so it would seem, Dutch paintings.

I was excited that my son wanted to see Van Gogh, so we went to the Philadelphia Museum of Art. There was the *Sunflowers* painting, just like *Baby Einstein* said.

Secretly, I was more than a little excited; my second degree was in art history. It must be a right brain, left brain thing—chemistry and art history. Nice combo.

We stood there with Van Gogh for a few minutes as a family, then we moved on to the next gallery, then the next gallery, then the next gallery. Minutes passed us by as they do in the slow motion of museum time. We were running zone defense that day; Renée had Mark's and Jack's hands, and I was responsible for Scotty. About five galleries into our ramble, Renée looked at me with an anxious expression.

"Where's Scotty?" she said.

The blood drained from my face. "I don't know."

"I've got these two. Go find Scotty!"

I zoomed around the Philadelphia Museum of Art for what seemed like ten minutes. I was running from this gallery to that gallery, almost to the point of yelling "Scotty!" when I slid into the Van Gogh room like Kramer bursting into Jerry's apartment, and there he was, staring up at *Sunflowers*, transfixed.

The moment was surreal. I could tell something was different. To say he was engaged with that painting would be an understatement. He was transformed. Thank God, there was an angel on my shoulder whispering, "Don't mess this up, man. Don't screw this one up."

I didn't say a word. I kept my distance and waited. I pulled out my phone and quietly snapped a few pictures. I even got a video of him studying the painting and starting to move away, and then he twisted around on one foot to re-engage. I kept moving closer and closer until eventually he turned to me, and we locked eyes.

"Scotty, why did you leave us?" I asked.

"Because I'm looking at the painting."

"I know, honey. We all looked at the painting. But you left us. You can't do that. Why did you leave us?"

He pointed at the painting. "I wasn't done looking. That's *Sunflowers* by Vincent van Gogh, my favorite artist. It makes me feel good when I look at it."

I'd never thought of myself as one of those sappy dads. Things didn't affect me . . . but that day I was deeply touched. Van Gogh reached through the canvas, across continents and decades and death, and he touched my child. And he did it by creating an experience that was 100 percent Vincent van Gogh, 0 percent *meta.*

"Daddy, you forgot to take my picture in front of *Sunflowers,*" Scotty said in a sweet and unassuming voice. He looked different. It's still one of the photos I will always treasure because I could see a part of my son I had never seen before.

Scotty was changed because he was part of an experience that Van Gogh created in 1889. He connected and he engaged, but he had to steal space (from me) to do it. He took that space, and he was transformed, but he had to take the necessary steps to make it his own experience. Granted, Renée and I took the kids to the museum, but the mere act of transporting children to a place isn't the experience. It's just part of it. Without knowing it, Scotty was at the center of a transformational experience that touched his heart.

✳

What did I learn that day? I don't create connections; my job is to create *opportunities* for others to make their own. Secondly, when emotions and physical experiences mix, the outcome is a moment in time so powerful that it can change the way you see, feel, think, and react forever.

Over time, Scotty became Scott. (I still get to call him Scotty.) He graduated college in 2024 with a degree in environmental science. I know . . . you thought art history, right? On graduation day, we found ourselves sitting on the steps leading up to the beautiful abbey where the ceremony would take place. Scotty and Mark were posing for photos in their gowns.

"Hey, Dad," Scotty said. "Check this out."

He lifted his pant legs to reveal a pair of *Starry Night* socks.

"I thought you'd like that," he said with the innocence of that seven-year-old I found standing by himself in front of Vincent van Gogh's *Sunflowers*.

Tears rolled down my face. The kid got it, and I was forever changed. Magic.

When we create an experience with someone else in mind and allow them to breathe and make it their own, they give us the gift of engagement. In my world, we call that the *best day ever*.

Best day ever moments happen when we connect and engage at the highest level. I am not an artist in the way Van Gogh was an artist, so I can't speak to that. How he set the table and created an experience for a seven-year-old a century later is beyond my ken. But he answered my question about *meta*-ing, because what happened to Scotty was only possible because Van Gogh was completely Van Gogh. Your authentic self will either connect or it won't; a fake self will only trick and fool. That's a false experience, which leads to a false connection. You're worth more than that.

The Lesson

- Authenticity can't be faked. If the experience doesn't matter to you, it won't matter to them.
- People don't connect with polish alone—they connect with purpose. Let them see why it matters to you.
- Engagement comes from resonance, not optimization. It's not about making the moment perfect. It's about making it meaningful.
- When leaders are emotionally invested, it gives others permission to care too.
- Great experiences aren't engineered solely from data; they're crafted through emotional connection and vulnerability.

PART 2

THE HARD PART: ENCOURAGING CONNECTION

In high school, Steve convinced his future wife, Renée, to take their science show on the road, bringing hands-on experiments to schools in Littleton, Colorado.

In the early years of his speaking career, Steve annually visited over a hundred schools to bring his traveling science show to students across the country.

News anchor and longtime friend Mark Koebrich gets an up-close lesson with one of Steve's earliest science toys—the legendary SQUIDY™.

In the early years of Steve Spangler Science, Renée transformed their living room into the company's first shipping center.

The famous Egg-in-the-Glasses trick—a classic demonstration of Newton's Laws of Motion in action.

Steve's parents, Bruce and Kitty Spangler, perform a routine called Magic Moments from their touring show.

Meteorologist Kathy Sabine teams up with Steve on stage to unleash the explosive reaction of Mentos dropped into a bottle of Diet Coke.

The original Mentos and Diet Coke eruption aired on Denver's NBC affiliate in 2006, launching a viral science sensation.

Giant rings of smoke soar into the crowd during STEM Day at Coors Field in Denver, turning science into a stadium-sized spectacle.

Professional development with Steve is full of surprises—especially for those in the front row.

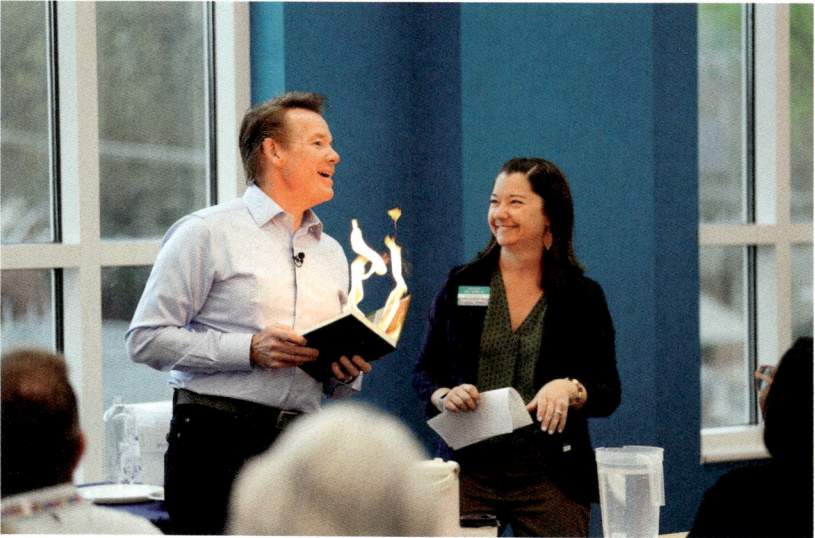

The flaming book made a dramatic appearance during one of Steve's keynote presentations—when science met storytelling with a spark.

Steve had a special guest appearance on *Side by Side with Nido Qubein*, which aired on PBS in North Carolina.

Meteorologist Janice Dean didn't expect Steve to light her hands on fire—especially not when she was filming live on national television.

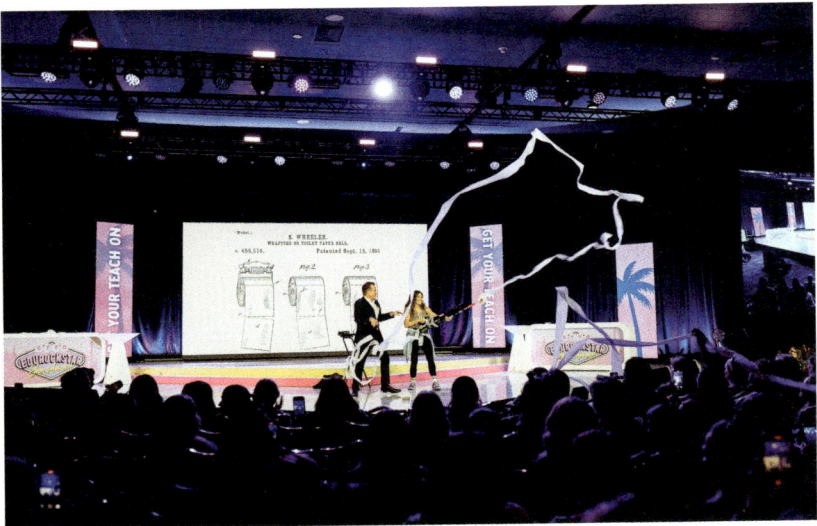

Steve shows his audiences the ultimate method for TP-ing anything— armed with a high-powered leaf blower and a burst of creativity.

The Mentos Geyser Tube toy made its explosive debut at the 2007 New York Toy Fair, turning heads with a clever—and controlled—way to launch soda indoors.

The Be Amazing Toys exhibit attracted buyers at the Toy Fair in New York with its hands-on science and eye-popping demos.

A behind-the-scenes look at one of Steve's hands-on science workshops, where teachers discover practical strategies to make learning unforgettable.

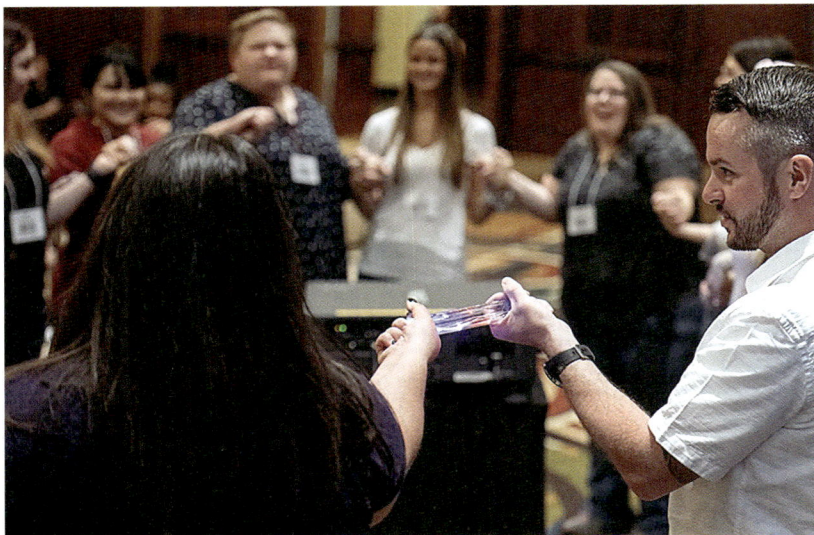

Audience members join hands to become a human conductor of electricity using the Energy Stick™ toy.

Hope King isn't sure what Steve had in store for her on stage at the Get Your Teach On conference.

For Steve's grand finale, flying rings of smoke blast through the air, toppling cups from the heads of audience volunteers.

It's an explosion of color as the audience taps into the power of air during Steve's signature Windbag experience.

Steve and Ellen DeGeneres fire up leaf blowers and unleash a few thousand Ping Pong balls into the audience—now, *that's* what you call audience engagement.

Steve lights up the stage—literally—as flames shoot from his wallet during his 2010 Speaker Hall of Fame induction speech.

Steve's Energy Stick is a safe and engaging tool that shows how circuits are formed using your body as a human conductor of electricity.

While walking the red carpet at the Daytime Emmy Awards, Steve and Renée paused for a quick photo—complete with the iconic flaming wallet.

The world's largest and messiest card trick performed on national television.

Steve with Ellen DeGeneres after whipping up a perfect batch of slime.

Teachers celebrate a *best day ever* experience with Steve Spangler.

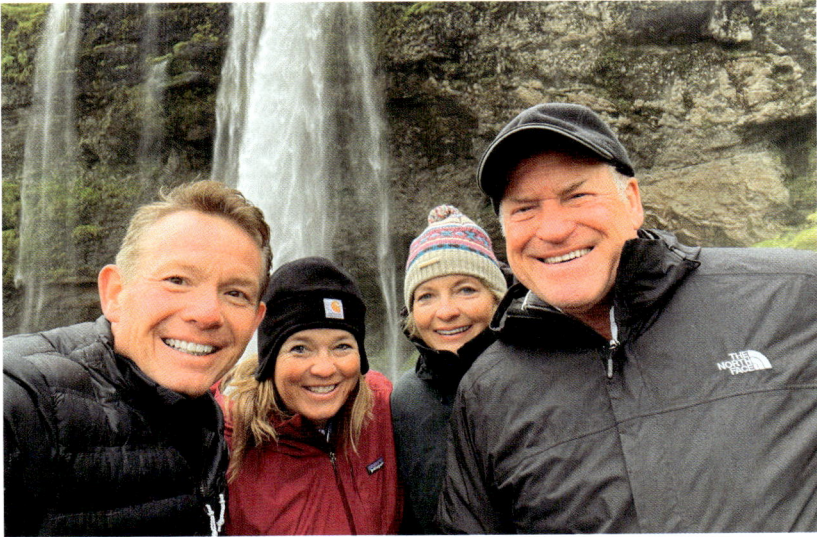

Steve and Renée explore the wonders of Iceland alongside their great friends, Sue and Mark Scharenbroich.

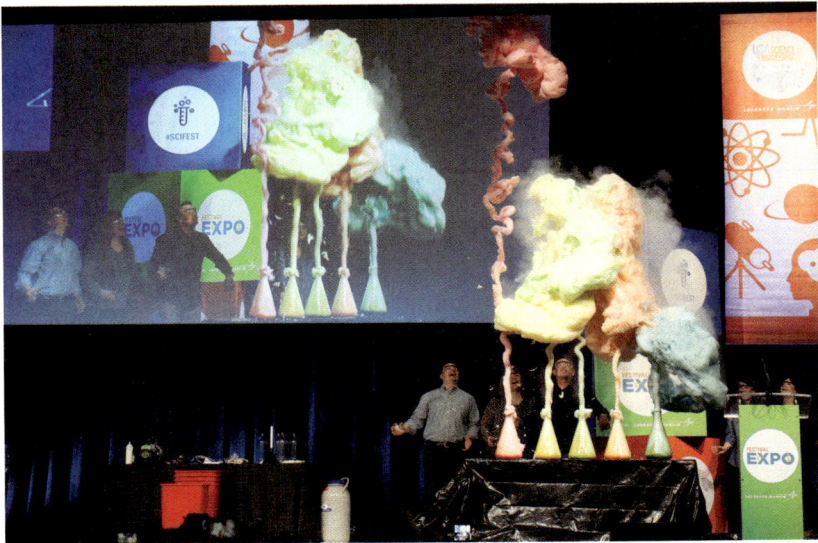

The famous Elephant Toothpaste experiment demonstrates the rapid
decomposition of hydrogen peroxide to produce an eruption of foam.

Teachers on the Science at Sea cruise study the impact of climate change on Margerie Glacier in Glacier Bay, Alaska.

Carly Reed rallies the Science at Sea participants in Ketchikan, Alaska.

In a rare onstage appearance, Carly Reed is surprised
to learn an explosion is just moments away.

In 2009, Steve set a Guinness World Record for the Largest Physics Demonstration by turning a simple science experiment into a record-breaking spectacle.

Steve delivers the opening keynote at the 20th annual Science in the Rockies conference, kicking off three days of hands-on STEM learning.

Steve wrapped up his first appearance on *The Ellen DeGeneres Show* with his signature Trash Can Smoke Ring routine.

Teachers dive into hands-on engagement strategies during an interactive Everyday STEM workshop experience.

Educators from around the world wrap up three unforgettable days of learning, laughter, and hands-on science at the Science in the Rockies conference.

Steve's liquid nitrogen cloud explosion performed at the Colorado Rockies STEM Day in front of fifteen thousand science enthusiasts.

On the set of the *DIY Sci* television series with Steve and his special guest, Miss America 2020, Camille Schrier.

The Ellen DeGeneres Show was the perfect play-ground to create larger-than-life experiences.

With more than fifteen thousand spectators, Coors Field in Denver became the ultimate classroom for the annual STEM Day event hosted by Steve and the Colorado Rockies baseball team.

Workshop participants get a one-of-a-kind perspective as they become the center of the action—launching over two hundred soda geysers in a single, unforgettable experiment.

Sometimes the most unforgettable moments come with the biggest mess—like this epic soap bubble explosion on *The Ellen DeGeneres Show*.

CHAPTER 15

THE NOTES IN BETWEEN

WHEN MY BOYS WERE GROWING UP, FAMILY VACATIONS WERE A combination of wish-list destinations and the number of frequent flyer miles in my account. The boys were approaching teenhood when Renée was able to pull off a most memorable vacation to New Orleans. Years prior, a teacher had given me the suggestion to take my family to Preservation Hall. Situated in the heart of the French Quarter, it would be the perfect place for my boys to experience their first actual jazz concert.

You stand in line outside the club, half a block off Bourbon Street. It's New Orleans, so everything's kind of damp. Finally, they shuffle you into Preservation Hall. It smells kind of damp in there too. It's a small club, the size of a nightclub, which I guess is what it is.

We walked in and sat down. The venue was small . . . so small our front-row seats put us within arm's length of several of the musicians. For an uninterrupted hour, we heard the most beautiful jazz. Most of the musicians were old guys, masterfully playing their drums, stand-up bass, piano, and sax. There was also a trumpeter who looked a lot like Louis Armstrong. It was eerie, like a time machine.

Our twins were ten years old at the time. That's young for an hour of jazz, but they were locked in like little jazz aficionados. We were sitting so close to the trumpeter that we could feel the air blowing out through his horn. When the set was over, the boys wanted to shake hands and thank the musicians for the music. The musicians stood in a receiving line on the way out the door, collecting handshakes and tips. The boys shook the old guy's hand; he still held his trumpet in the other.

"Thank you very much, sir."

"Thank you, young fellows."

When it was my turn, I said, "Thanks for a treat tonight."

"Thank you, young fellow." I was forty-three.

"Hey," I said. "I think you've been doing this a while. What keeps you coming back?"

"Probably not the money, right?" he said.

"Right," I said. "Probably not."

"It's the notes in between."

Sometimes someone says something to you that you don't understand, but the gravitas of it hits you like a brick just the same.

"Forgive me. I'm not a musician," I said. "I don't know the *notes in between*. What does that mean?"

"Every night," said the trumpeter, "I know where the song's going to start. And every night, I know where the song's going to end. But I never know what's going to happen in the middle. We call those the notes in between. Those notes happen because the audience is there. You help craft the notes in between." He looked right at me, possibly through me. "Young man, you helped us create some great notes in between tonight."

I shook his hand again. I didn't want to leave him, but there was a line of tourists behind me, plus Renée and the boys were waiting in the damp street.

I walked out into the French Quarter thinking, *Oh my God, the notes in between. What an amazing metaphor for everything in my life.*

I know where I'm going to start. I know where I'm heading. But the way we get there, the route, even the character of the final destination—it's all about the people around me. It's the space I allow for connection. Wow, I gotta sit down.

I don't know if the trumpeter was an oracle or if that was a canned answer he gives to anyone who asks, but it clarified leadership and connection for me in a profound way.

As a teacher, I know where I'm starting a lesson, and I know where I have to finish it, but the beauty and the joy of discovery and learning are in the ups and downs in between—and that's dependent on who's there, my interaction with them, and their responses. It's in the space in between that we connect.

It's in the space in between that we connect.

Jazz gives some musicians hives because it requires them to go off-score, to let someone else lead, to relinquish control, to give and adjust and give and adjust. I've heard people say jazz is about showing off virtuosity, but I think it's deeply generous music. Music about giving.

Jazz is a beautiful example of what connection looks like when it flows from a shared experience. At its best, jazz is *always giving* in real time. An orchestra gives its audience a painstakingly arranged symphony. That's a beautiful gift. But the trumpeter gave us his notes phrase by phrase, as each moment demanded. I can't imagine a more exhausting kind of music to perform—another reason it reminds me of teaching children.

✳

Is connection possible without a shared experience? No.

Is engagement possible without connection? Absolutely not.

Connection is the cornerstone.

At a higher human level, connection is about love. It's about not being alone in the world. It's a shared moment with someone who looks nothing like me, who doesn't speak my language, who wouldn't even notice me if we passed on the street, or who I wouldn't notice myself. By creating a shared experience and leaving space for that person to connect (as opposed to waiting for that person to applaud), I leave room for the notes in between.

"Steve, chill. I smell the campfire. I see the single tear cascading down your cheek. This is supposed to be a leadership book. What's this got to do with me?"

I'm glad you asked. Though I do believe in connection as a way of life—as a spiritual practice, if you'll allow it—I have also learned that it is essential for cultivating engagement in those I lead. Whether it's in the classroom or from the stage or on the screen . . . no connection, no engagement. A great leader creates an experience, then waits for those they serve to accept the invitation to connect.

If you're a leader, you're probably really good at the control part. Super. The letting go part can be a challenge. Here's why: You can't fake it.

For a connection to work, for it to be a legitimate connection at all, you have to leave room for the other person to choose and steer. *They might say no.* If true connection and engagement are what you want, you have to steel yourself for that possibility. You cannot force it. If you could, it wouldn't be a connection. It would be uncomfortable.

I know I'm going to lose the control freaks here—along with the lion tamers, the dictators, and the leaders who lack trust. You will be displeased with most of what follows. But you have to learn to connect collaboratively if you want to connect at all.

The Lesson

- Connection doesn't always come from what you say—it often comes from the space you leave for others to say something back.
- Silence is powerful when it's intentional. It invites reflection, emotion, and the opportunity for others to step into the experience.
- The best moments of connection happen in the unscripted pauses. That's where people process meaning and find their place in the story.
- Relinquishing control allows others to participate. That participation makes engagement mutual, not just a performance.
- Like jazz, connection requires improvisation. You may know where you're headed, but the real beauty comes in how you get there—together.

CHAPTER 16

CONNECTION IS TWO-WAY, OR YOU'RE JUST PERFORMING

F YOU DON'T ALLOW ROOM FOR CONNECTION, IT CAN'T FLOW IN BOTH directions. And if connection isn't a two-way street, it's not really a connection at all. It's just a show.

Long before slime became trendy in toys and education, I rolled into a second-grade class with my A/V cart to teach the kids my favorite recipe for making slime. My goal was to teach a little chemistry.

I showed the kids some finished slime first because you have to get their attention.

"I'm going to show you guys how I make this stuff," I said. "It's like this."

I started making the slime, and then this boy—who was a pretty ornery kid, the kind of student who typically doesn't engage at all—said, "Wait just a second."

I stopped pouring the watered-down Elmer's Glue into the measuring cup. "Yes?"

"I need a pencil and paper." He turned to his teacher and said, "Ms. Moore, I need a pencil and a piece of paper ... right now."

You could hear a pin drop. All the other kids were giving shifty glances as if to say, "I've never seen him write anything down."

The kid got his pencil and paper, and said, "OK, now what was that again? Half a cup of warm water?"

Every other kid started digging for their own pencil and paper.

"Hold on, Mr. Spangler," someone else said. "I need to write this down too."

I had been performing, but that ornery kid was telling me to make room for him. He wanted to connect and engage, but I had to slow down and get the heck out of his way. That connection transformed him into a totally different student, suddenly attentive and curious. That got everybody else's attention and made them want to get in on it too.

The same thing happens in a business setting. Every presentation and every project are opportunities to connect—if you are willing to go off-script and make room for the other people at the table. I got lucky that day because that boy cared enough about making slime to tell me to slow down. You might not be so lucky. More often than not, folks will just let you put on your little show while they tune you out. It's up to you to leave room for them to connect—and maybe to provide pencils and paper.

STEVE'S SLIME RECIPE

Making slime is nothing more than learning how to connect long chains of molecules. Lucky for you, Elmer's Glue is a perfect source of long chains of molecules. The secret ingredient you'll need to find at the grocery store is borax (you'll find it in the detergent aisle).

Ingredients

- Elmer's Glue (8 oz.)
- Utensils: large mixing bowl, spoon, measuring cup, plastic cup (the 8 oz. size works well), teaspoon
- Warm water
- Food coloring (the spice of life)
- borax powder
- Resealable (Ziploc-style) sandwich bag (don't you want to keep it when you're done?)
- Paper towels (hey, you've got to clean up!)

The measurements do not have to be exact, but it's a good idea to start with the following proportions for the first batch. Just vary the quantities of each ingredient to get a new and interesting batch of goo.

This recipe is built around a brand-new eight-ounce bottle of Elmer's Glue. Empty the entire bottle of glue into a mixing bowl. Fill the empty bottle with warm water, replace the cap, and shake. Pour the glue-water mixture into the mixing bowl, add a drop or two of food coloring, and use the spoon to mix well.

Measure half a cup of warm water into the plastic cup and add a teaspoon of borax powder to the water. Stir the solution—don't worry if all the powder dissolves. This borax solution is the secret linking agent that causes the Elmer's Glue molecules to turn into slime.

While stirring the glue in the mixing bowl, slowly add a little of the borax solution. Immediately you'll feel the long strands of molecules starting to connect. It's time to abandon the spoon and use your hands to do the serious mixing. Keep adding the borax solution to the glue mixture (don't stop mixing) until you get a perfect batch of Elmer's slime. You might like your slime stringy; others like theirs firm. You're the head slime mixologist—do it your way!

When you're finished playing with your Elmer's slime, seal it up in a resealable bag for safekeeping.

The Lesson

- Engagement is not a solo act. When it's one-way, it's performance. When it's mutual, it's a connection.
- People want to contribute, not just consume. Give them the opportunity to shape the experience with you.
- The best leaders and communicators make space for response. They don't just deliver a message; they invite participation.
- Connection requires vulnerability. You have to be willing to let the audience influence the moment.
- Engagement that sticks is cocreated. It's built on shared ownership of the experience.

CHAPTER 17

MORE INTERESTED THAN INTERESTING

I AM GENUINELY INTERESTED IN PEOPLE. FANATICALLY SO. THAT HAS only intensified through years of practicing experience, connection, and engagement. So there, I've said it. I'm a connection addict. Hand up.

But there is another reason I learn a waiter's name or ask the nice lady at the bus station about her eyelid piercings: practice. It keeps me in practice.

We've all been around people who we hope will ask us just one question. People who must be the star of the show at all times. People who interact as though the rest of us are bit players in their feature film. They want to be more *interesting* than *interested*. It's exhausting for the rest of us, and it makes for very poor leadership.

Engagement is one of the many things in life that works great when you try it backward. Being more interested than interesting is engagement in reverse. If you are interested (*actually* interested) in another person, there's a way better chance they reciprocate with a connection.

This whole premise came to me from my mentor, Mark Scharenbroich. Mark often cites Barbara Jordan as the one who said, "It's more important to be interested than interesting." He first heard her say it while watching her being interviewed on *60 Minutes*, and it left a lasting impression. The same quote is also attributed to Dale Carnegie, who wrote in his classic book *How to Win Friends and Influence People* that one should "become genuinely interested in other people."[18] It's sound advice, no matter who said it first. I cite Mark.

Mark Scharenbroich is a highly acclaimed motivational speaker and the author of the book *Nice Bike: Making Meaningful Connections on the Road of Life*. The premise begins at the 2003 Harley-Davidson company's hundred-year anniversary celebration. Thousands and thousands of bikers throughout the world attended the event. Mark isn't a Harley guy. He doesn't own a Harley. He's never even sat on a Harley. But Mark is insanely curious, and he is a wonderful observer. As a Harley owner stood proudly by his bike at that event, what two words from a passerby would have made their weekend? That's right: "Nice bike."

"It's more than a casual compliment," Mark explains to his corporate audiences. "It's the engine that is fueled with the three actions of acknowledging, honoring, and connecting with others. "When you have a better understanding of how to make meaningful connections, you can live a life filled with a greater sense of self-worth and accomplishment in your work and in your life."

Mark totally gets it. I've never met anyone who has a better grasp on what it takes to make meaningful connections with other human beings. So I decided to heed his advice and take this "nice bike" thing out for a spin. My speaking calendar keeps me on the road about a hundred and fifty days per year. That means I have lots of time on lots of airplanes. As chance would have it, one day I was on a flight back to Denver with a seasoned pilot in the seat next to me. We struck up a conversation about aviation, busy airports, and his career as a pilot.

"How can you tell if your copilot is any good?" I asked.

"It all comes down to the landing. Pilots take great pride in being able to give their passengers the perfect landing, where the wheels just kiss the runway.

"Landing in Denver is tricky even for seasoned pilots," said my new pilot friend. "Let's see how this guy does."

Beautiful landing.

On my way off the plane, I poked my head into the cockpit and said, "Which one of you is responsible for that *nice landing*?"

The first officer turned around in his seat, straightened his shoulders, and said in that pilot voice, "That would be me." His smile said it all.

The Nice Bike Principle works. With two simple words, I acknowledged, honored, and forged a new connection, even just for a fleeting moment. Best of all, it felt good.

Now it's your turn to try it. Be on the lookout for a meaningful way to connect with a complete stranger. You won't believe how well it works.

Thanks, Mr. Scharenbroich.

Welcome to My Life, Tattoo

I don't have tattoos. I came into this world uninked, and I'll probably leave this world the same way. I've found tattoos to be a fantastic way to connect with people—because they're intensely personal, yet totally outward-facing. That's the perfect setup. They're remarkable inroads for asking about someone's story.

"Your sleeve looks different from the last time I ate here. Did you add something?"

Nine times out of ten, their mouth says, "I did," and their eyes say, *Whoa, you saw me.* That's huge. That's powerful.

Is it a little contrived? Sure. But it works. Tattoos themselves are only mildly interesting to me—but the people inside them? They're fascinating. Asking about someone's sleeve is reverse engagement—an outward gesture designed to invite connection.

"Did you design that? What does it mean?"

They always have a story. They always tell me something about their life. The door instantly opens to something better: I get to learn a little bit about *them*. Now we're connecting. Another bridge of trust is built in the world, even if it's built on one simple conversation. The connection is the purpose; the tattoo is just the catalyst.

Learn to look for a catalyst. It's the flame wallet, the shrimp and grits, the slime, the tattoo. Whatever it is, seek an opening.

Learn to look for a catalyst.

"I love your pink hair. When did you decide to do that?"

At one point, early in our adulthood together, Renée asked me directly, "Why do you do that?"

"Do what?"

"Why do you get into every stranger's life?"

When the boys became teenagers and saw other, quieter adults moving through the world, they, too, thought it was strange.

"Dad, you don't have tattoos. What do you care?"

"I care because I'm interested in what makes people tick. I care about connecting. Plus, they always have a great story, right?"

"Hey, Dad, can I get a tattoo?"

"Talk to your mother about it after you turn thirty."

Lunch Lady Land

Early in my speaking career, I was visiting a little more than one hundred schools per year. I did this for thirteen years. I've seen lots and *lots* of gyms and school cafeterias. While the person who brought me in to speak was usually an administrator or maybe the PTO president, I interacted the most with the school secretary, the custodian, the gym teacher (since I hijacked their space for the day), and the wonderful people who served lunch.

"Word on the street—food around here is good." I've said this to cafeteria workers since those early years. "I hear the kids really, really like the thing you do with the tater tots."

This is made up, sort of. It's a game, but it's a game that invites the staff to be their best selves. My line is bogus, but my interest is legit.

"Everyone's talking about lunch. What's the deal on Fridays?"

Two women and a guy. Hairnets, aprons, the whole attire. The guy says, "We do some special things on Fridays." You can see him puff up a little bit. It's the same reaction I get when I use Mark Scharenbroich's Nice Bike Principle.

"What's the secret?"

"You eat with your eyes first," he says. "Our food always looks great."

Pay dirt! I just learned something interesting from someone who takes pride in his work. He feels good, I'm learning, we're liking each other. Connection made.

"Where'd you learn that?"

"Culinary school."

"Forgive me, but did you go to culinary school for a cafeteria job?"

"Oh no, no," he said. "I had a great job at a pretty high-end restaurant for a long time. But I got tired of making great food for snotty people. Now I make great food for appreciative kids."

I think you can tell a lot about a person by looking at two things: the way they treat service people and the way they treat animals. For somebody to be at lunch and not acknowledge a waiter, not at least stop talking long enough to ask their name . . . it blows my mind.

Of course, I push it further. When Fred the waiter's not all that busy, I'll stop him. "How long have you been doing this? How do you serve a thousand meals in an hour?" Open the door, and they'll tell you.

It irritates my companions from time to time. "Oh, it's just Steve doing his shtick." But I wanted my boys to see it. And now I'm starting to see them being more interested than interesting. It's essential for a leader to nourish this skill, and I think it makes the world a better place to live.

On a practical level, it can even make life easier. For example, I do not follow sports. Does that mean I don't engage with sports people at holiday parties? No, it does not. I stand there and talk football with them. Not with any insight. I don't have a lot to contribute. But I can at least listen and ask them questions.

"What happens when somebody in your fantasy league is killing, and people are pissed off?"

"Do you use AI when you're making draft picks?"

All I have to do is ask something like that, and a half-hour discussion ensues, usually with a decent story attached. At the end of the night, everybody walks away feeling pretty good. We get to toast one another: "When we were all standing around drinking mojitos, waiting for the turkey to cook, I really had fun talking ball with you."

I didn't talk much. I listened a lot, and I deliberately engaged. I didn't go sit on the couch like a bump on a log. That is the self-sacrifice element of connection. Just like jazz, it's all about giving.

Two Acknowledgments

Acknowledgment 1: What I am describing is connection for its own sake. The tattooed lady, the cafeteria guy . . . I am not these folks' leader. I am not trying to build capacity in them to reach their highest potential (though I hope they do). I'm just a curious guy with a connection addiction. But like I said, it's also good practice for me, and it's an energy exchange that can improve everybody's life . . . or at least their day.

Acknowledgment 2: To some people, this tactic seems like a hoax. I understand, but I respectfully disagree. The real difference between asking someone about their tattoo and asking them how it's going is that I actually want to hear what the other person has to say. Which one is the hoax?

I challenge you, Dearest Gentle Reader, to try this for thirty days. Engage first. Start that conversation. Be interested in somebody. Make it about them, and you almost always learn something. Whether it's a lunch lady or a cabbie in New York, everybody's got a story to share if you choose to engage.

We were at the grocery store recently. I was looking through shampoo. I turned to the lady next to me and said, "Is this shampoo any good?"

"Hmmm, I really don't know."

"Well, what do you get?"

She started talking. By the end of it, I knew her dog's name and that her son was an econ major at the University of North Carolina.

Shy Renée still laughs at me about this habit. "You can come up with something to say to anybody, can't you?"

"Absolutely."

"Did you really care what that lady wanted in a shampoo?"

No, but that's not what it was about. This habit teaches me how to talk to others. Am I ever going to see the shampoo lady again? Probably not. But that moment helped me become a better communicator. It was practice. On the flip side, it gave her a moment as an authority. For most of us in leadership roles, that is an area in which we need all the practice we can get. Even though Renée is much more reserved around strangers than I am, she still gets how powerful connection can be when you apply these principles to the team you depend on. She explains:

> When people ask us why our employees stuck around for years at Steve Spangler Science, I tell them it was because the boss asked them for advice. We engaged the employees. We didn't take every suggestion, but we always asked. That goes a long way because it puts the spotlight on them while the responsibility stays on us. Just because you engage doesn't mean you're deferring authority, but people feel more connected when you respect them and the things they know. And that connection is powerful. It also helped us out on more than one occasion.

People are canny. People are clever. When we finally figured out that we weren't the smartest people in the room, everything got easier. When we had the confidence to engage our employees and even our vendors—all the people who were smarter than us—we did so much better. The key was connecting by asking.

You can't know everything. Not about shampoo or cafeteria lunch or even your own business. Leaders who can acknowledge that will add superpower after superpower with every staff member they have on board. And it all comes from the pursuit of connection.

The Lesson

- Curiosity is the fastest way to connection. People lean in when they feel you're genuinely interested in who they are and what they have to say.
- Great leaders ask better questions. They don't need to have the answer; they just need to make others feel valued and heard.
- Listening is more than waiting for your turn to talk. When you listen with the intent to understand, you build trust.
- Being interesting draws attention. Being interested builds relationships.

CHAPTER 18

SEEN AND HEARD

Mrs. Sanders, a teacher in Denver Public Schools, reached out to one of the producers of our television series (*DIY Sci*) to ask if we would be interested in helping her make science fun for her students. She had seen episodes in which we visited schools to work with teachers to create some of those unforgettable experiences. It's always a fun challenge. Fast-forward a few months, when we brought *DIY Sci* to her school to try a little experiment.

Most of the kids spoke only Spanish ... and this science guy speaks only English. That was our first challenge. What's more, these fourth graders seemed to be scared to death of the gringo with the rapid-fire English and the trunk full of crazy experiments. If our goal was to create an experience in which the children felt safe to engage and learn something new, we needed more than a flaming book or flying toilet paper to build those connections.

We decided to craft a lesson around movement, with a chance to sneak in a few things about Newton's Laws of Motion.

All good experiments start with a question. In this case, the question was, "How do you make the perfect glass of chocolate milk if you don't have a spoon?"

You might answer, "Stir it with your fingers."

Gross. No. Try again.

How about finding a way to swing the glass of milk around in the air to stir it up without spilling a drop?

Perfect!

It's a good experiment, but we had to tackle our challenges first. The kids couldn't understand me, and they didn't totally trust me.

I had to enlist the help of our host teacher, Mrs. Sanders. The students already trusted her—and she spoke Spanish. When she, my newly enlisted cohort, suggested my solution to her students, fear and excitement welled up in their eyes in equal measure.

I pulled out a simple contraption I'd made in my garage. It was a thin wooden tray about a foot square with pieces of rope tied to each of its four corners. I filled a few plastic cups with water and carefully placed them on the tray. With the tray suspended by the ropes, I began to swing it back and forth, each swing getting a little higher. The kids were silent, but their eyes were wide open.

"See, the cups stayed on the tray," I told the kids as a few of them started to applaud. "And we didn't spill a drop." I gave it a few more swings, then decelerated until the tray hung by the ropes again. "Would anyone like to try?"

There were no takers, but a few of the students immediately pointed to Mrs. Sanders. The idea quickly gained momentum.

I didn't expect that response, but it sounded like a good idea. I racked up another tray of cups, but this time, I added a few more, each one filled to the brim with water. Some of the kids squealed with delight. Others took a few steps back.

Mrs. Sanders held on to the ropes tightly as she rocked the tray of cups back and forth.

"*Más alto!*" the students chanted. Higher!

That's when I yelled, "Swing it over your head!" and pantomimed it. Mrs. Sanders looked at me in disbelief.

"*Hazlo!*" the kids shouted. Do it! Their voices grew louder and louder.

And then it happened. She swung the tray completely over her head, just like swinging a bucket of water, and she didn't spill a drop . . . until she was mobbed by her adoring fans with hugs and high fives.

Quick aside: The magical moment I just described wasn't planned that way. The original plan was for me to do the trick and then offer a student the opportunity to try it. But something unexpected happened. The children offered up their teacher as the sacrificial lamb (so to speak). They could see she was nervous. The moment was real. She was doing what each of them secretly wanted to do but was afraid to step up and do themselves.

In the end, this little experiment built trust between me and my twenty-three new best friends. I never could have guessed how important it would be for the students to see how I interacted with the teacher they adored. No embarrassment or humiliation. Mrs. Sanders was the star of the show. The kids were ready for anything. Mission accomplished, and we were just getting started. I reached into my trunk of wonders and pulled out a dozen more swinging tray contraptions and a giant stack of plastic cups.

"Now, who wants to try it?" I asked.

They couldn't believe we were letting them . . . especially with cameras rolling. We quickly moved everyone out to the playground because things were about to get messy. Twenty-three centripetal force trays spun around like a bunch of drunk galaxies. Some of the young Einsteins got it right away, while others sent their cups of water flying through the air. The kids' joy was palpable and immense. They were so excited. The camera guys were enchanted by one little girl in particular.

"Steve, look at her."

She had absolutely blossomed. She was pure joy, spinning the tray in every direction possible, chattering away to nobody in particular. It was all Spanish, so I had no idea what she was saying. Mrs. Sanders had to go over to translate. We got it all on camera.

"What are you doing?" asked the teacher.

The girl was almost emotional. "I didn't think I could do it! I didn't want to do it! But Mrs. Sanders did it, and I knew I could do it, and I did!"

It was all her. She didn't do it for anybody else. She didn't try to get anybody else's attention. She was in a moment of joy because she had been given an opportunity and had been left to act on her own. She was transformed.

That's transformational engagement. I had seen it in my own kid when he did the Van Gogh thing. That's what I saw in this girl's eyes.

When kids have that moment—when they realize the cups stay on the spinning tray—anyone can recognize that it's the personal discovery that brings them such great joy. That's when they start to teach themselves. That's engagement. It only happens if you make it about them, and it's only about them if you make them feel seen and heard—and then get out of the way so they can choose to connect.

It has become a manipulative cliché for a manager to say, "I see you. I hear you." Don't patronize people. Verbal acknowledgments can be important, but seeing and hearing are acts. What happened with the little girl and the spinning tray would not have been possible if we had assumed the language barrier would hinder connection. Good leaders see and hear their teams to build them up.

Good leaders see and hear their teams to build them up.

Connection Frames an Experience with Significance

Dr. Nido Qubein taught me how to see and hear a team.

Dr. Qubein is a master of creating extraordinary experiences—an educator, entrepreneur, and visionary who has transformed High Point University (HPU) into what he calls *The Premier Life Skills University*. Since becoming president in 2005, he has reimagined what higher education can be, turning HPU into a place where students don't just earn degrees but also develop the mindset, skills, and confidence to thrive in a competitive world. His vision is built on the idea that education isn't just about information; it's about inspiration. He believes that every interaction, every environment, and every opportunity should elevate students, helping them see what's possible and giving them the tools to make it happen.

Under his leadership, HPU is more than a university. It's an *experience* designed to shape leaders, innovators, and problem-solvers who understand that excellence isn't an accident; it's a choice. I credit Dr. Qubein with the phrase, "Frame the experience with significance." It is a mantra he lives by.

I am fortunate to be part of the *Access to Innovators* program at HPU. This program brings global leaders and innovators to campus, providing students with unique opportunities to learn from and interact with successful individuals across multiple industries. Steve Wozniak (Apple cofounder), Marc Randolph (Netflix cofounder), Cynt Marshall (Dallas Mavericks CEO), and Dr. John C. Maxwell (renowned leadership expert) are just a few of the experts who are available to HPU students and faculty as part of the *Access to Innovators* program. This exposure broadens their perspectives and inspires them to think ambitiously.

I conduct interactive workshops and seminars where students actively participate in experiments, transforming abstract concepts into tangible experiences. Beyond workshops, I mentor students on STEM projects and career paths. My goal is to exemplify Dr. Qubein's commitment to providing students with extraordinary educational experiences that not only impart knowledge but also inspire and transform. A tall order, but the man inspires confidence!

If you plan to walk the HPU campus with Dr. Qubein, prepare to meet some young people, because students are attracted to him like paper clips to an electromagnet. They routinely go out of their way to see him, even walking across a courtyard simply because Dr. Qubein is on the other side. And it's not because he's giving away chocolate (though he usually is).

I've known Dr. Qubein for many years as a fellow member of the National Speakers Hall of Fame, and I'm honored to serve as adjunct faculty at High Point University as their STEM Educator in Residence. Whenever I visit HPU, he still insists on taking me to dinner. He relishes the opportunity to engage and ask questions. And when I watch him take a real interest in the people of High Point University—from the students to the custodians to the professors to the shuttle drivers—it inspires me to be better to those in my orbit.

Several years ago, I was on campus as part of a business leaders' retreat. Dr. Qubein led our group of twenty or so people on a tour of the campus. We were talking, talking, talking, as speakers do. He was listening, listening, listening, asking questions, being quietly wiser than the rest of us combined. Doing Nido stuff.

We were walking through one of several student centers on campus when Dr. Qubein excused himself from the group. He walked over to a custodian who had just finished cleaning the men's bathroom. They spoke for less than a minute, and Dr. Qubein rejoined our group. No one said anything; we weren't quite sure what had just happened. Did he see something that wasn't to his liking? Was there an issue with this employee? Dr. Qubein resumed the tour as if nothing had happened.

But curiosity got the best of me, and I just couldn't help myself. I broke away from the group and walked over to the custodian.

"Hi, my name is Steve," I said. "I know it's none of my business, but are you OK?"

"I'm Walter, and I'm doing just fine," the gentleman said as he continued to organize supplies on his cart. "Is there anything I can do for you?"

"I'm on campus with a group of businesspeople, and we're learning about how things work here at HPU. I couldn't help but notice Dr. Qubein stopped our tour to come over to talk to you. Did you get in trouble?"

"Oh . . . that? Dr. Qubein always makes it a point to come over to tell me how much he appreciates how I take care of this school. He says I treat it like I own it."

Then I asked the question you're probably supposed to just think and not say out loud.

"Did he just do that because we're here?"

"No, he stops to talk whenever we see each other. That's just who he is."

Our tour made a stop at one of the cafeterias. Dr. Qubein announced it was lunchtime, and we were to get anything we wanted from the myriad shops. Since HPU is a cashless campus, he told us the employees knew who we were and anything we wanted was on his tab.

"Can we at least put a tip in the jar?" one of the guys in our group asked.

"We don't have tip jars. Just smile and tell the cashier something you liked about the shop. I'll see you back in the meeting room in an hour. Oh, by the way," he added, "I'd suggest sitting at a table with students. Ask questions. Be curious."

Our group split up and did exactly as Dr. Qubein had instructed. It must have looked like parents' weekend had come early as we awkwardly looked for a place to eat. I got lucky. It was almost as if these kids knew I was coming to their table. There were three students at the table, two girls and a guy.

"You're welcome to sit here," said one of the girls.

The first thing that caught my eye was *their* eyes. All three students were looking at me. No one had their phone in their hand; no one was scrolling through their Instagram feed at lightning speed. The young man stood up when I started to sit down. He extended his hand to shake mine.

What is going on? I couldn't help but feel a splash of suspicion as these students . . . well . . . *initiated* engagement with me, a stranger on their turf who was more than twice their age.

The girls also shook my hand as they launched into their first round of questions.

"What brings you to campus?"

"I'm here with Dr. Qubein for a business leadership retreat."

They just smiled. The questions kept coming. They wanted to know where I had been, what I had seen, and where I wanted to go. One of the girls wanted to know more about me and my business. Seriously, it was easily ten minutes before I had a chance to ask my first question.

"OK, my turn. Who taught you to do this . . . to act this way?" I blurted without thinking of a better way to say it. "Who taught you to stand up, shake hands, look me in the eyes, ask meaningful questions, and put your phones away? I know you all have phones, but I haven't seen you touch them at all!"

I think my question caught them off guard because they didn't have a good answer. This is just part of the culture at HPU.

High Point University's focus on life skills began in 2005 with the arrival of Dr. Qubein. Today, students learn the value of building meaningful connections and choosing to engage. They learn that everyone wants to be seen and heard, that everyone has a story to share, and that everyone has something important to teach—if we choose to listen.

After only a day at this week-long leadership retreat, I could have packed my bags and headed home; these amazing students gave me a master class in the art of creating transformational experiences. My lunch hour was nearly over, and I needed to speed walk back to the meeting room.

When Dr. Qubein welcomed us back, one of my colleagues raised his hand.

"Dr. Qubein, many of us are wondering about your interaction with the custodian back in the student center," he said in a tone that suggested he *knew* what was said during the conversation. "Clearly, there was an issue with something you saw—something that didn't meet your standards—and we were impressed that you *dealt* with the issue and your employee away from us."

"I appreciate your thoughts on this, but that's not at all what happened," Dr. Qubein said with a little laugh in his voice. "I just stopped to see how my good friend Walter was doing."

I almost blurted out, "That's right! The custodian's name is Walter! He knows his name!"

Instead, I kept it to myself. I sincerely believe Nido stepped away to connect with Walter because that's just the person he is. People choose to care and connect on the deepest level when they feel honored and acknowledged.

✳

You'd better believe the bathrooms are clean at High Point University. It's not because of threats, and it's not because of manipulation. It's because the entire community there feels valued, and they feel valued because they *are* valued. That begins at the very top, with Dr. Qubein.

When people are met where they are, when they are honestly seen and heard, when they are allowed to make their own choice to connect, most will. Whether you're spinning a cup on a string or cleaning a bathroom or running a university, those are the touches that create a culture of engagement. There is no other way.

The Lesson

- Recognition isn't optional; it's foundational. When people feel seen, they begin to show up in new ways.
- Something as simple as calling someone by name can be transformational. Visibility builds belonging.
- Engagement begins with acknowledgment. When people are affirmed, they're more likely to lean in and contribute.
- As leaders, our job isn't to be the loudest voice; it's to notice the quiet ones and invite them in.
- Being seen and heard is about identity, not ego. It tells someone they matter.

CHAPTER 19

TRUST THEM

THE GREATEST SALESPEOPLE IN THE WORLD WILL ADVISE YOU TO GIVE the customer some time. Back off a little. "You know what? Maybe this car isn't for you." Show them something else. To be clear, you're not threatening to take away the car they want; you're giving them the opportunity to choose for themselves. No amount of convincing can compare.

Carly uses a similar approach when she's working with a potential client who is wavering in their decision to formalize an agreement for a keynote presentation. "You know, there's a possibility Steve may not be a good fit for you and your goals for this event. Let me send you the names of a few speakers you might want to consider."

This is 50 percent sales tactic and 50 percent "set Steve up for success." Carly knows the experience falls short whenever we try to force a square peg into a round hole. I love Carly's approach. Take a step back, give the potential client some time to think, and let them reengage if and when they're ready. If I'm the right fit, they'll be back.

*

I should acknowledge again that the scary part for business folks is taking your hands off the wheel and letting people choose to connect. If I do exactly what I'm supposed to do as a teacher—as the leader—my student is going to find the groove on their own. I've created the experience to get their attention and build capacity in them. Now I have to let them choose to connect. Can't force it. This comes down to trust. It will be, by far, the most difficult thing for some people, especially the hardcore alpha neurotics. If that's you . . . I see you. I hear you.

Teachers sometimes send me footage of their classes doing the wacky stuff I taught them at Science in the Rockies or some other workshop. I love this. The very best videos show a kid putting their own spin on something, doing something totally new, something I'd never thought of—out-wackying my wacky. Classrooms full of kids trying to outdo one another, trying to awe their teacher, pushing an experiment to its limits, and dazzling themselves when it works... these are the most vibrant, fertile classrooms. Productive chaos. Abundant engagement. Magic.

Now try to make that kid do a worksheet. Never in a million years. But he can hardly wait to tell people about what he figured out on his own. Activities are transactional; experiences are transformational. The magic is in the freedom of allowing people to drive. You let them figure it out, and then everybody in the room is present and engaged.

More often than not, I bring someone onstage during my keynote presentations or teacher workshops and use an Energy Stick as a metaphor for building connections. But I prefer to push it. I give each table an Energy Stick and tell them to try it.

"Just pass it around. It won't work with more than two people."

That's a setup. I'm secretly begging them to try it with more than two people. Eventually, one table does it with three, and then they try it with their whole table. I pretend I have some legitimate business to take care of onstage. I turn my back on the audience to fiddle around with something. In about thirty seconds, people and Energy Sticks start squealing as people try greater and greater numbers. By the time I'm back on the mic, we've got three hundred people rung around a conference hall making one Energy Stick sing. Everyone is a kid again. And just like kids, their brains are firing because they figured it out themselves.

After doing this hundreds of times with audiences of all ages, I've learned the importance of giving the audience time to explore and make their own discoveries. I've had audiences turn on me when I tried to wrap up the activity too soon.

"No way! We're not done yet!" yelled a man in a three-piece suit.

I looked in his direction. Frankenstein and his lab assistants had turned their table into a giant electrical circuit. They discovered that cloth napkins became great conductors of electricity when they got them wet, and that baby carrots conduct electricity better than copper wire. The completed circuit was a labyrinth of silverware connected to remnants of mashed potatoes, peas, chicken, peach pie, and a trail of asparagus leading back to the other end of the Energy Stick. The camera guy ran over to the table, and the A/V team put it up on the big video screens that flanked either side of the stage. The moment the asparagus tip touched the other end of the Energy Stick, the circuit was complete, the gizmo flashed and made noise, and the entire ballroom erupted into a standing ovation. High fives, hugs, mic drop.

I'm convinced these moments happen for a reason. It's the Universe teaching me to give the learner the tools they need, let go, and trust them to drive. My goal was to use the Energy Stick to illustrate a lesson in the power of building connections. But by simply letting go and creating space for the learners to explore on their own, creativity abounded, and new, unpredictable connections were made.

I would be wrong not to acknowledge the elephant in the room. "That's cute, Steve. But time is money in my business. I don't have time to wait for my team to get with the program and make their own discoveries. It's keep up or get out."

Fair enough. But if you think your team members are less of an asset than your time, I suggest you're leaving most of your business's potential on the table. Every situation is different, but I hope you would consider at least trying this engagement strategy. I've seen skilled managers use the technique masterfully. And (just as I did) they got way more bang out of their participants than they ever could have expected.

✳

Get the setups right and trust them to find their way. Let it happen. A brand-new teacher doesn't even know what those three words mean because they're usually way too scared to trust the kids. It's the same with a first-time boss most of the time. But in every successful experience I've described so far—Scotty and the Van Gogh, Science at Sea, the girl and the swinging cup—the common factor is that people were given the freedom to connect for themselves. Imagine if I had said to Scotty, "Find a moment alone and go stand before *Sunflowers*. You're going to feel something. Go engage." That would have been a disaster.

A friend of mine once had a boss who bounced from office to office, telling her reports how much better she would be at each of their jobs. My friend quit. Everybody did. Trust is hard in any case; trusting those who look to you for leadership may be the hardest thing of all. After all, you're the one in the big chair. It goes without saying that you would be the best at everyone's job if there were only more of you. (If only!) Right . . . ?

There is a better way. Imagine your team is full of surprising gifts and energies that only they can tap into, and only if they choose to tap into them. Imagine your job as the leader is to lay the groundwork for that tapping: to up their confidence, to take a bunch of distractions and tedium off their hands, to trust them to bring their best selves to bear on the tasks at hand.

Maybe you need to spin it as trust in your own process, in the efficacy of the experience you created. Whatever. Spin it however you need to spin it if it helps you shut up and get out of the way.

The Lesson

- Trust builds the foundation for growth. When people feel believed in, they take risks, try harder, and invest more.
- Micromanaging sends a clear message: "I don't trust you." It shuts down creativity and invites disengagement.
- Great leaders give enough structure to guide, but enough freedom to explore. That balance empowers others to own their work.
- Delegation isn't just about efficiency—it's about belief. When you hand off responsibility, you communicate confidence.
- Trust is more than just a leadership tool. It's an invitation to collaborate, grow, and connect at a deeper level.

CHAPTER 20

FEIGN IGNORANCE

OMETIMES, THE LINE BETWEEN EXPERIENCE AND CONNECTION GETS fuzzy. Same with connection and engagement. Connection has one foot in experience, one foot in engagement, and . . . a third foot? A tail? Nope—forget that.

Here's the real takeaway: When you strip everything down, experience and connection can happen at the same time *if* the setup is simple and you leave room for it to unfold naturally. And one of the best ways to do that? Act like you don't know something—ask for help you don't actually need.

I do this all the time with kids.

"Hey, do you like mac and cheese?"

Of course they do. Kids love mac and cheese.

"Look, I'm not great at making it. What's the best way to do it? The *absolute* best way?"

Boom. Now they're talking. Do I care about mac and cheese? Not really. But I care about getting them to open up. It's like an old magician's trick—except instead of sleight of hand, I'm using curiosity to pull them in. It's not full engagement yet, but we're moving in the right direction. If I had a big vat of something they could stir, pour, and experiment with—boiling points, solubility—we'd be *there*.

But even in the mac and cheese conversation, it's about connection. If you want to build a connection, the only thing you can do is extend an invitation. You can't *force* connection, but you *can* make it irresistible. And I'd be lying if I said my mac and cheese hasn't improved based on what I've learned from seven-year-olds.

The Zoom Trick

Sometimes I run a Zoom conference for seven hundred teachers at once. That's seven hundred people I have to connect with—through a webcam. And I have *fifteen seconds* from the moment Carly says "action" to grab them.

How do I start?

"We made it! It's December! How many more days until winter break? Throw it in the chat!"

Like clockwork, my screen will explode with comments. Because teachers *always* know exactly how many days are left before winter break—down to the millisecond.

"Thirteen days left! I can't wait!"

"Thirteen days!"

I'll say, "Thirteen days! You've worked so hard. Tonight, I just want to look into this camera and say thank you. I hope for the next hour, you can breathe and relax a little. Your students are going to *love* what I'm about to show you, and I guarantee you'll come up with even better ideas than I have. Drop them in the chat so we can all see."

Now there's a workshop happening *inside* the workshop.

I can't read hundreds of comments while I'm presenting, but Carly's scanning them, pulling out the gems, and feeding them into my earpiece. It's like holding today's newspaper in a ransom photo—proof that I'm actually here, live, and listening.

Carly whispers, "Rachel says you should add food coloring to the borax."

I say, "Did you guys see what Rachel just wrote? Holy cow, that's *brilliant*! Why didn't I think of that?"

And just like that, the spotlight moves to someone else while I take responsibility. Rachel is at home thinking, *He saw my comment. He said my name.* And that's a big deal.

I tell teachers this all the time: I know you know your subject. But your students? They don't care how much you know. You shouldn't be trying to impress an eighth grader. Be *real* instead. Let your ego sit this one out and make it about them.

Let your ego sit this one out and make it about them.

"I never thought about connecting the circuit that way."

That's the goal. Because if you want kids to truly engage—to lose themselves in the experience—feign ignorance. If your goal is to get them to admire you, well . . . that's a whole other conversation.

The Fear Factor

This technique is not new. Parents have been doing it with their toddlers since toddlers were invented. But I still get resistance to it—especially from teachers of older students and managers who struggle with confidence. Their fear usually sounds like this:

"If they think I don't know, it makes me look like an idiot."

But it *doesn't* make you look like an idiot. It makes you look *human.* And honestly, who cares? Is teaching about you, or is it about them?

The Lesson

- Curiosity is one of the most underrated leadership tools. Asking questions—especially when you know the answer—can be a powerful signal of respect.
- Pretending not to know can lower defenses. It creates space for others to step forward and share what they know, which deepens ownership.
- People are more engaged when they feel like contributors, not just spectators. Playing ignorant (authentically) invites others to fill in the gaps.
- When you model learning instead of certainty, you invite collaboration and build trust.
- Great leaders don't always need the last word. They know the value of silence, listening, and learning in real time.

CHAPTER 21

THE PART ABOUT ELLEN

T HE *ELLEN DEGENERES SHOW* GAVE YOU A PAIR OF BRANDED UNDER-
wear after each appearance. I have twenty-seven pairs of *Ellen*
boxer briefs.

Being on *Ellen* changed my life. It also taught me a lot and
confirmed a few hunches about how experience, connection, and
engagement translate at the highest levels.

Be Visible

I joined the National Speakers Association (NSA) in 2000. The
NSA is the leading organization for professional speakers—keynote
presenters, trainers, and thought leaders who use the power of words
to inspire and educate. Since 1973, the NSA has helped speakers
worldwide sharpen their craft and grow their influence.

For the first seven years of my membership, I attended all the
summer conventions and participated in the winter workshops, but I
didn't speak once. By that, I mean I didn't put my name in a proposal
or offer to host a breakout session, and of course, I was never invited
to present on the main stage. Compared to most of the attendees, I
was a ghost.

If you've never been to a convention for professional speakers, I'll save you the trouble: It can be exhausting. Attention and stories are currency. Talking shop is literally just talking, from sunup to sundown. It is a celebration of extroversion. It's as fun as it is loud—and it is very, very loud.

Sometimes, the best way to handle those situations is to sit back and let them play out before you. Differentiate yourself by shutting up. There's so much noise, you'll lose your voice trying to be heard. Best to stay mum.

But in 2008, I was invited to the main stage. It wasn't out of nowhere. My videos on a relatively new website called YouTube were gaining traction, and some members knew about my decade of weekly appearances on the NBC affiliate in Denver. But all of that paled in comparison to my big break . . . the *Ellen Show*.

I worked for months on the nuts and bolts of my presentation, "From Exploding Soda to Flying Potatoes: The Science of Unforgettable Engagement." The keynote was a nice mixture of engagement strategies that speakers could use with their audiences and a few eye-catching science experiments to keep everyone on their toes. Yet as the big event grew closer, I got the sense from the conference organizers that while they *liked* the science stuff I pitched, they would *love* it if I talked more about my recent *Ellen Show* appearances.

Hmmm, I thought, *I see where this is going.*

In a moment of pure inspiration, Carly wrote my opening line: "It's amazing how many new friends I have at NSA after being on the *Ellen Show*." That got a laugh.

"So many of you have reached out," I said. "You all have such incredible stories to tell. And you all want my contact at *Ellen*. And you want to know how I got on the show. Ladies and gentlemen, I am going to tell you how. If I were you, I'd take out a pen and a piece of paper. I'm going to give you the secret."

A rustle of paper in the audience. The chitter of clicking pens.

"I asked my producer at *Ellen* the best way to have you reach out to him. And here is his answer. I have it on a slide."

I clicked the slide. Two words appeared: *Be visible.*

You can actually hear eyes narrowing when fifteen hundred pairs of them do it at once. Before they could get their pitchforks out, I told them the truth about how it happened for us.

We didn't have a PR agent pushing us. We didn't send *Ellen* a press pack. One of their producers—and there are probably forty of them—was following my weekly segments on 9NEWS (the NBC affiliate in Denver), and he signed up for my Experiment of the Week email. Every week in his inbox, he would get some simple experiment like the balancing nails or the self-crushing can. One day in a pitch meeting, he said, "I watch this science guy. Ellen might have some fun with him." The idea got shelved. And then it came back around again. And then we got the call.

It was the quietest I have ever heard an NSA convention hall. Maybe that's because I'd never heard it from this side of the podium, but I'm not convinced. From the mic, it sounded dead quiet.

"After all the attention we got," I said to the speakers, "I did reach out to the producer for you. 'Listen, I've heard from a ton of people. They want to know how I got on the show. What do I tell them?' He said, 'Tell them to do exactly what you did. Be visible. If we call you, it means you have something we need. We saw you do something that grabbed our attention. If you do that, you don't have to worry about pitching us. We'll come to you.'"

I wasn't exactly carried off the field in triumph, but neither was I burned at the stake. Speakers are smart. If they wanted a shortcut, they were probably disappointed; but they know a good hack when they hear one.

The Show Starts Before
the Show Starts

They hyped the audience for almost an hour before *The Ellen DeGeneres Show* actually began. To create the experience, they had to get these people primed long before Ellen came out. You could feel the bass from the music all the way backstage in the green room. Subwoofer speakers were even built into the audience's chairs. To this day, I can feel what it was like when the show started. The audience was live forty-five minutes before, and they danced like there was no tomorrow. A terrific comedian who got no airtime had already gone out and done a warm-up set. When Ellen finally emerged, the rush of energy was an earthquake.

But they'd had to work up to that point. They had to prep people to the point that they were going to lose their minds. They had shaped the experience right from the start in such a way that people would feel comfortable losing themselves in the moment. When the curtain opened, the audience was primed and ready to go.

Fake Engagement Is a Disservice

Ellen and I always had a legitimate shared experience onstage, and that's what people liked. That's also the reason the other talk show science people have a hard time trying to replicate (OK, I can say *steal*) the experiences we were able to create together. It's easy to copy the flying toilet paper bit or the ten thousand Ping-Pong balls. But you can't re-create the way those moments in time made the audience feel.

I don't want to overstate our relationship, but Ellen and I had an organic connection during the experiments. No matter what we were doing, people wanted to see us experience it together, and they couldn't wait to find out what I had in store for Andy (only the *real* Ellen fans will understand this).

The reason it felt so authentic was that Ellen suspended her control so that she could be genuinely surprised. She refused to find out in advance what was going to happen. That awes me to this day. I was there to create a little world, and she was willing to walk into that world blind, just like any hyped-up audience member. We always did rehearsal with a producer who stood in for Ellen (many times, it was Andy) because she wanted to preserve a sense of wonder. She didn't want to fake it. That was why it worked.

The secrecy was serious business. If we were working on a really big experiment backstage, they would put up a wall of pipes and drapes so Ellen wouldn't see it when she walked by. She didn't want to do a disservice to her viewers by knowing about a surprise ahead of time. She was their proxy onstage. She wanted a real reaction.

Please recognize the enormous amount of trust she put in her team and ours. That's also why the producers were so careful to vet everything I was going to do—especially the stuff that required Ellen's direct participation.

In one of my first appearances, we filled bubbles with a mixture of hydrogen and oxygen gases. Ellen and I put on our safety glasses and earplugs before she scooped the bubbles into her bare hands. Then, I touched a lit match to the bubbles. The explosion was deafening. Now you know why we had ear protection . . . and the audience could feel it in their chests. The expression on Ellen's face was a combination of astonishment and the *I-will-kill-you* look I got from her from time to time. Pure gold. The audience went nuts because the emotion of the experience was genuine. That shared experience between the two of us became a running gag throughout the next fifteen years of appearances on the show. All I had to say was, "Remember the exploding bubbles?" and the audience would laugh because Ellen would give me the look.

The producers weren't sure if she was going to lie down on the bed of nails, but she didn't want to know ahead of time, so they had a stand-in from the audience at the ready.

"If she says no, we've got somebody from the crowd you can use."

All that was behind the scenes. It was extra work for everybody else and extra risk for Ellen, but it was worth it to her. She wanted to create an authentic experience for her audience. It paid off. And yes, she lay on the table, I pushed the button, and forty-five hundred nails lifted her body six inches off the surface. The audience went wild.

Be Decent

When I did the *Ellen Show*, there weren't a lot of people doing talk show science stuff. There had been a few on Johnny Carson many, many years before. Lee Marek did it on *The David Letterman Show* in the 1990s. Don Herbert, better known as "Mr. Wizard," had been on and off TV since the 1950s. Bill Nye's popularity grew throughout the '90s, but even he would rarely do a live experiment. The *Ellen Show* was the beginning of talk show producers on the prowl for nerdy scientists with loud, over-the-top demonstrations.

The very first time I was on *Ellen*, the set was a tight seven minutes. Our first interaction was scary for me because I didn't know how she was going to react. Does Ellen like science? More importantly, would she like a nerdy science guy in his forties? Our first bit together involved a balloon filled with a mysterious gas. I invited her to breathe in the gas and then talk. Of course, the audience thought the gas was helium and her voice would have a high pitch. Much to everyone's surprise, the gas was sulfur hexafluoride—a gas six times heavier than the air we breathe. When she spoke, her voice sounded like Darth Vader . . . and her comedic timing was perfect.

"Luke. . . I am your father," she said.

The surprised audience laughed, and in that laughter, they gave me permission to build a connection with *their* friend, Ellen DeGeneres. While I'd like to think it was me selecting a great first experiment, the truth is I made a lucky choice, and Ellen set me up for success.

As we were leaving the stage, one of the executive producers, Andy Lassner (yes, *that* Andy), came up and put his hand on my back. It was September 2007.

"Hey, great job," he said. "Don't do *The Tonight Show*, and we would love to have you back in November."

"Oh, I've never done *The Tonight Show*," I said.

"Give it two weeks or so. They'll call you. You're going to say no or you're going to say yes. It's in your court. They've seen you here. They liked the chemistry."

My head was spinning.

"Mark my words," he said.

Two weeks later, we got the call from *The Tonight Show*. Jay Leno was hosting at the time. One of their human-interest producers called.

"Hey, we've been thinking science, and your name popped up. We would love to have you on the show."

"Thank you so much," I said. "But I am really happy with the *Ellen Show* right now. I think I'm going to keep doing that."

There was a pause, then the guy said, "Good job. You have a good thing going. Just keep doing that show."

Jimmy Kimmel's casting people put out a request for proposal for a Steve Spangler–style science demonstrator to all the Hollywood agents. My agent at William Morris Endeavors sent me a text saying, "Kimmel wants a Steve-Spangler-like science guy."

The next time I was on the *Ellen Show*, one of the producers showed me the RFP.

"Look," they said. "They're trying to copy our Weird Science segment . . . but what they really want is someone who connects with the host. They're looking for chemistry . . . and that's hard to find."

During the commercial break, Ellen mentioned how other shows were hunting for science people.

"I know you could do other shows," she said. "Thanks for being loyal to us."

Whatever we did on *Ellen*, two months later, other shows would do the same thing. If I used a red trash can, they'd use a red trash can. If I had a blue blowtorch, they would use a blue blowtorch. If I told a joke, they would use the same joke. Imitation is the sincerest form of flattery, and I remain flattered that they liked what we did with Ellen. But even now, years after the end of the *Ellen Show*, they keep missing the legitimate connection that made the segments work.

The senior producer (whom I had the good fortune to work with for many years) sent me a clip of another science demonstrator doing the exact "gag," as they say, on a daytime talk show. His only comment to me was, "The segment is flat. There's no connection. They're just doing stuff you'd see at a weak science fair. The audience doesn't care. The magic is the connection!"

Keep It Real

I remember the day we did the flying toilet paper experiment. In short, I taught the viewers how to turn an ordinary leaf blower into a high-powered toilet paper launcher. This thing could empty a roll in fifteen seconds flat. My motto has always been "anything worth doing is worth overdoing," so we filled the stage with sixty-four leaf blower contraptions ready to shoot toilet paper.

To get her involved, the producers said Ellen should push a button that triggers all the toilet paper shooters to go off. They had to bring in 640 amps of outside supplies to power the blowers that shot the toilet paper. There was an electrician backstage turning it all on to make them fire at once. Of course, the electrician had to flip the real switch, so they gave Ellen a fake button. The audience helped me with the countdown . . . 3 . . . 2 . . . 1 . . . She pushed it, everything went off, and that was that. It looked amazing. The stage and the first half of the audience were completely covered in toilet paper. No one had ever TP'd a talk show.

Ellen found out after the fact that her button had been phony.

She asked my segment producer to only give her real buttons from then on. "If you give me a button," she said, "I want it to control something!"

Ellen also never used me as the butt of a cheap joke. I was never the goofy scientist. Other television talk show hosts make fun of their science people. Producers dress them in dumb lab coats with goggles and stupid gloves. Even their introduction is demeaning.

"Well, Phil the Discount Scientist is here with more experiments from his science garage guaranteed not to work."

The science person is always the joke.

Ellen never wanted that. She was truly enamored with the science. In fact, the notes I would get back from the producers were, "Next time, do a little bit more science. It's OK to explain. We'll give you a little more time." I didn't have to wear a lab coat or pretend to be something I wasn't. What a dream.

Our very last segment together was in May 2022. I had thought it was going to be my appearance the month prior. But during a commercial break, Ellen said to me, "You've been on how many times?" (She knew the answer.)

"This is my twenty-sixth time on the show, and I'm so grateful you kept inviting me back," I said.

"How would you like to make it twenty-seven? Only two other guests have been on more times than you," Ellen said with what I felt was gratitude in her voice. "Let's do one more."

"Do you have any requests . . . a favorite experiment?" I asked.

"Destroy the place, as far as I'm concerned. It's been a fun ride," Ellen said as the music started to play, and the red light came on.

Our last segment was so much fun . . . and a little sad for this science guy. Ellen's final show aired on May 26, 2022, and my last appearance was just two weeks earlier. The producers were kind enough to give me a few seconds to tell Ellen thank you on the air. I never thought I would get emotional over a television show, but this was more than just TV. She was special. If she liked it, the rest of the world liked it.

The giant doors opened, and as promised, we went out with a bang. Ellen was so kind to invite Renée and my three boys and Carly to join me onstage, along with all the backstage people who had helped us pull off the larger-than-life experiments over the past fifteen years.

Picture a dozen large barrels with soapy water and a splash of neon paint. Everyone was dressed in hazmat suits as we prepared to dump liquid nitrogen (-320°F) into the water. When the two liquids mixed, the soapy mixture turned into what can only be described as monster foam that covered the stage. Maybe that's why everything was covered in plastic.

Again, you can't force connection. You can't force engagement. My time on *The Ellen DeGeneres Show* worked for so long because it was allowed to be organic and unforced. They had the resources to allow us to do things bigger than we had ever dreamed. But the magic of the segments—and the reason it worked over and over and over again—was Ellen's decision to relinquish control so that genuine connection could be possible. There is no other way. She knew that, and millions of people connected through her.

Thanks, Ellen.

The Lesson

- The bright lights don't change the basics—authentic connection still matters most.
- Preparation and humility are the foundation of memorable moments.
- Just because the stage is bigger doesn't mean the message should be louder—it means it should be *clearer*.
- Success on national TV is built on the same principles as success in the classroom, the boardroom, or the dinner table: trust, timing, and a willingness to take risks.
- Even in high-stakes environments, personal connection creates the most impact.

CHAPTER 22

INVITE THE BEST VERSION

HAD TO GET NEW TIRES LAST WINTER. BLECH. CARLY SUGGESTED I try Jake's Tires because they had done a really good job for her. Every time I take Carly's advice, my life improves, so I headed to Jake's.

Mechanics wear shirts with their names on them. I love this. When I walked into the front office at Jake's, I noticed the name *Blair* on a guy heading back into the garage.

"I'm looking for Blair," I said.

Blair was gone, but there were a couple of employees in the office.

"Is there something I can help you with?" said the guy at the desk (whose name tag, I kid you not, read *Smitty*).

"Here's the deal," I said. "My colleague Carly, who's been with me now for twenty years, she won't let anybody else touch her car besides you guys. I need tires, and I heard there is absolutely nobody on this planet who does tires better than Blair."

The other guys' posture changed completely. They're in the repair business, so they expect folks to come in pissed or impatient or in despair, demanding attention. I had turned the spotlight on them, and everything shifted.

"Carly said Blair did the best tire job she's ever had in her life," I said. "So I'm here for Blair."

I made most of that stuff up. Carly did say Jake's was a good place and had a good price. But the last thing I'm going to do is walk into a mechanic and say, "I heard this place is cheap."

Somebody went to fetch Blair. He came into the office looking bewildered. Smitty was looking at him like he had never seen him before.

Blair shook my hand.

"What can I do for you, sir?"

"What's your secret, Blair?" I asked. "I heard you were the best."

"Well, I just, you know . . . I just know the cars." He stood up a little straighter.

"How long you been doing this?"

"This will be my eleventh year."

"Well, no wonder," I said. "Will you come out and take a look at my tires? Somebody told me I should be getting new ones."

Blair came out and looked at my tires.

"Your friend was right," he said. "You need tires, sir. Relax. I know exactly what I'm putting on."

That was the moment Blair took the reins. He didn't ask my budget. He didn't ask my preferences. He saw that I had confidence in him, and he took control of his work. The worst thing I could have done at that moment was ask Blair about prices or something. Let Blair cook.

✳

I acknowledge that this is unusual behavior. Many people will never be comfortable walking into a tire shop and putting on a little theater to boost their confidence. I know that, and I don't want you to think it's a shortcoming. I was deep in my teacher bag when I singled out Blair. Plus, as I mentioned at the beginning of this book, I'm a connection junkie; I love sharing moments with people, and I love to see others thrive.

But please recognize this as a matter of scale: It was easy for me to defer to Blair because I know nothing about tires. I invited him to be the best version of himself, and I gave him the opening to rise to the occasion. It's exactly what I do when I tell people the Energy Sticks only work with two people. I don't have to feign ignorance about tires, but I still have to set the table for others if I want to give them the opportunity to thrive.

To get ahead of a potential scruple: This technique will not bestow someone with qualities they do not possess. If Blair had been hopeless with tires, I would have been sunk. But I had enough context to take that risk. I would not, on the other hand, pull a drunk out of the pub and say, "I've heard you're the best babysitter in town!"

※

Carly was right: I did get a deal at Jake's that day. When I went to the desk to pay for my (amazing) tires, Smitty asked if I was one of their club members.

"No, I'm not a club member," I said.

"You are today."

He acknowledged me because I had acknowledged him and his guy. There was a mutual connection there. That was a nice benefit, but not one I was looking for. Give without remembering, receive without forgetting.

One caveat: Blair did a super job on my tires. But if Blair had blown it, I could not march back into Jake's with an axe to grind. That would be entrapment. There is always risk when you delegate. There is always risk when you trust. If you're a leader, that's part of the job. Leaving room for connection means leaving room for disappointment. Picking people back up when they fall is part of the gig.

When somebody acknowledges you and honors you, you want to be better. But we should lead with kindness, even when we're disappointed.

When somebody acknowledges you and honors you, you want to be better.

The Lesson

- People tend to live up to the expectations we set—especially when those expectations are tied to their potential, not their past.
- Creating conditions for someone to succeed often means stepping back and giving them the room to rise.
- A leader's belief in someone is often the invitation they need to believe in themselves.
- You don't need to orchestrate every moment. Sometimes your role is to quietly hold the space where growth can happen.

CHAPTER 23

RESONANT FREQUENCY

Allow me a labored metaphor. It appeals to me as a science guy. If you set a steel plate over a loudspeaker and pour salt over the plate, the salt will begin to dance, organizing itself into astonishing patterns depending on the frequency you send through the speaker. You should try it. Don't use your own speaker. Wait until you're invited to dog sit at a friend's home. The salt aligns itself, crystal by crystal, based on the frequency, then realigns itself into another pattern when you shift: square wave, sine wave, 400 Hz, 30 Hz, whatever. They all have a salt profile. Magic.

The environment you create on the steel plate will send the same salt crystals from a circle to a triangle to a spiral. Same salt, same plate. The only thing that changed was the energy you sent through the speaker. In a week, you couldn't scrape those crystals into anything close to the patterns that they will organize themselves into if you just leave them alone with the energy you create.

I won't insult you by unpacking this metaphor. But I will emphasize that all you can do by trying to physically "help" organize the salt is screw up the pattern.

＊

My goal as a leader is to find the right resonant frequency for you, but the only way you're going to change is on your own.

My goal as a leader is to find the right resonant frequency for you, but the only way you're going to change is on your own.

If you've been in the leadership business long enough (teacher, administrator, manager, executive), you've probably noticed that people come up to you and give you credit for things you never did. It happens to me, as I'm sure it does to you. If not, wait a couple of years.

"You changed the way I teach in my classroom."

All I can say is, "You're so kind to say that. But I don't think it was me."

"No, really. You transformed it."

"No, really," I say. "*You* transformed it."

We were at a conference in San Antonio a few weeks ago. What a fun town. A teacher ran up to me on the River Walk and said, "Steve, I just wanted to thank you. You changed the way I teach. It was the thing that you did with the eggs."

"Seriously, that's just a trick," I told her. "How did that change your teaching style? I just showed you how to knock eggs into glasses."

"No, not that. It was the egg geodes."

"Really?" I said. "Turning an eggshell into a model 'geode' did it for you?"

The egg geode has way less razzle-dazzle than the eggs in the glasses. Less *ta-dah* focused on the teacher and more moments of *wow* for the students to experience. Never in a million years would I have ever put the egg geode experiment on my top 20 list, but I'm so glad she took it and ran with it.

On a personal note, I almost omitted this story about the Texan teacher from the book because of the way I responded to her kindness and heartfelt words. Instead of looking her in the eyes, pausing my banter, and acknowledging what she said, I immediately deflected the praise and tried to make it all about her.

"No, it's not me, it's you ... " Blah, blah, blah.

But that's not what she wanted or needed to hear at that moment. She needed me to accept her kindness and hear me say, "Thank you. That means so much to me."

Pause ... no talking ... smile ... and hug.

I learned this lesson the hard way. A good friend who had joined me for dinner was standing right there and heard the whole thing go down. After we walked away, he did what any good friend should do: He told me the truth.

"You're better than that," he said. "You needed to acknowledge and respect her words without deflecting the praise away from yourself."

He was right. I needed to give her the gift of gratitude by using two simple words: "Thank you." I'm still learning, and I hope you are too.

As a leader, you are the architect of the frame. Whatever happens, it happens within the confines of that frame. Your job is to create an experience in which your followers have the energy they need and feel safe from ridicule and distraction. You build capacity. They draw the picture on their own.

I know I'm repeating myself, but you can't read this enough: Leadership is service. The greatest achievement of any leader is the success of a follower. You can encourage that success by finding your people's resonant frequencies. (And don't forget to say thank you when that service is acknowledged.)

※

When a teacher finally learns how to craft experiences the correct way, there's a sense of calm in the classroom. That's because they have learned to let go so that connection can happen. The teacher trusts their energy, which means they can trust their students to move on their own. The same is true of a boss who does their job well.

Every salt pattern is like a fingerprint. It's like an individual kid. Our job is not to arrange them or change them; our job is to dial in on the resonant frequency that makes that kid move independently. A couple of hertz up, a couple of hertz down. Sometimes it's a matter of dialing through frequencies to find what resonates. They will usually tell you when you find it, like when that ornery kid stopped me in the middle of my slime presentation to ask for a pencil and paper. Sometimes you get lucky.

Beware! The twenty-three other kids *will not* all have the same resonant frequency. From a business standpoint, every employee is not going to resonate the same way. It's your job to dial in for each one as best you can. Does that sound like too much work? You're the leader! That's why they're paying you more!

You will notice that some salt grains refuse to conform to any pattern, no matter how many frequencies you throw at the plate. *C'est la vie*. If you can't figure it out, don't be afraid to ask. Even if you never nail resonant frequency with every single person (you won't), you can still invite them to be the best version of whoever they are.

The Lesson

- Resonance is about emotional alignment. When people feel you're tuned into their wavelength, trust and connection deepen.
- Communication isn't just verbal. Tone, timing, presence, and energy all play a role in how your message lands.
- People don't always remember what you said, but they remember how they felt in your presence. That feeling is resonance.
- The leader's role is to attune to the emotional frequency of the moment and respond with awareness, not just instruction.

CHAPTER 24

GABBY

M

Y FIRST TEACHING JOB WAS AS A ROVING SCIENCE TEACHER ON AN A/V cart. If you're under forty, you may not know what an A/V cart is, because A/V is now just called *life*. A/V stands for *audio/visual*. In the pre-smartphone, pre-laptop days, the equipment that made audio/visual things happen was heavy and cumbersome. It was also prohibitively expensive; many schools only had a few TVs or VCRs or laser-disc players (Google it), which meant they had to be mobile. The answer was a metal cart with two or three tiers and one wonky wheel whose approaching squeak still invokes video time for generations of children who are now old people.

Necessity is the mother of invention, so A/V carts became go-to storage and transport for anything that didn't have its own room at a public school. Sometimes it was art, and sometimes it was health. At Willow Creek Elementary in Englewood, Colorado, it was Steve Spangler's science class. Room to room I rolled, squeaky wheel announcing my arrival, to entice young minds with the wonders of science.

I would teach from the cart for eleven years.

*

Elementary school teachers hate Halloween. I love it. I love fizzing things and bubbling potions and fake blood and things that catch on fire. So in my second year on the cart, I went to our staff meeting a week before Halloween and said, "Hey, everyone, I have a Halloween science show I can bring to your classes on the cart."

The teachers perked up. They wanted Halloween to be over.

"It's about a twenty-minute show. If you want to sign u—"

I didn't even finish the words. That staff room turned into the trading floor of the New York Stock Exchange.

"9:15!"

"I'll take 9:45!"

"I want 10:30!"

Then, the mayor of the school (if you're a teacher and you don't know who the mayor of the school is . . . it's probably you) slowly raised her hand for all to see.

"Steve Spangler, I'll give you fifty bucks to do the whole day in my room."

I could feel the other teachers sending me telepathic warning: *Don't do it, man. Don't do it.*

I didn't take the fifty bucks, but I walked out of that staff meeting booked from first bell to dismissal on Halloween.

✳

Pushing an A/V cart filled with gizmos and gadgets through a classroom doorway can be a tricky maneuver. You couldn't get in the door cleanly, plus you were anticipated by the squeak, so there was no element of surprise. It was almost impossible to make an entrance. I needed to make an entrance on Halloween. Fifteen seconds. My solution was to twist the cart at a little angle and give the door a massive kick. *WHAM!* I might take out a kid, but they're resilient at that age.

At 8:15 a.m. on Halloween morning, I kicked open the door of Mrs. Ridgley's third-grade classroom, plowed the A/V cart in, and yelled, "Get to the back of the room!" The kids glued themselves to the back wall.[19]

There was a pumpkin on top of my cart. I had carved a jack-o'-lantern face and placed the shapes back into the holes. I dropped a few small chunks of calcium carbide into the pumpkin and added a splash of water for good measure. As the two chemicals mixed, the reaction produced acetylene gas. A little spark from a barbeque lighter was all that was needed to ignite it.

Click. *BOOM.*

The face flew out of the jack-o'-lantern, and the kids lost their minds.

Before their hysteria died down, I grabbed the 30 percent hydrogen peroxide (ten times stronger than your mom's remedy for scrapes and cuts). There was no TikTok yet. There was no YouTube. They had no idea what Elephant Toothpaste was. (Side note: Google "Elephants Toothpaste" to see why kids love this reaction. Or scan the QR code on page 84.) I poured the peroxide in, added the catalyst, and waves of foam oozed out of the eyes and mouth of our newly exploded jack-o'-lantern. Magic.

As it was made clear to me in the administrative hearing that followed, I should have put down a protective covering over the carpet since hydrogen peroxide does the same thing to carpet as it does to your hair. But that was neither hither nor thither on Halloween.

Next up on the ol' Halloween Science Show, it was time to learn about the chemical energy found in candy—sugar. I'm a chemist, right? If you put a gummy bear in a test tube, add an oxidizer such as potassium chlorate, and give it a little heat, the bear will start to smoke and release that energy. Nice demo. But remember, anything worth doing is worth overdoing, so I got a large Erlenmeyer flask (the glassware kind, in the shape of a triangle) and added a few heaping scoops of the oxidizer. That much oxidizer needs a lot of heat. That's why you need a blowtorch to do this right. Hey, it was 1992. No one cared. I liquefied the oxidizer with the blowtorch. The kids were pinned to the back wall, looking like the floor might fall out from under them.

The recipe called for one gummy bear. I reached into the bag for one gummy bear, but somehow my hand grabbed five. It seemed like such a good idea at the time. Halloween. Candy day. When I dropped those bears in, fire shot from the Erlenmeyer flask like a volcano.

The newspaper reported that Steve Spangler lit a kid's desk on fire. That's not true. A gummy bear that was *itself* on fire jumped out of the Erlenmeyer flask and landed on a kid's desk. Anyway, I didn't know what to do, so I grabbed a math book and slammed it down on the flaming gummy bear. The kids were dead silent. I looked at them, and they looked at me, and I said, "Don't tell your mom and dad."

My grandpa was a teacher in Denver Public Schools for forty-one years. Grandpa used to say, "Teachers make so much money they sometimes get a *second* job." I didn't get the joke when I was a kid, but I laugh every time I think about it today. That's why Grandpa and Grandma owned an antique store in Denver. Grandpa had the coolest toys. My favorite was this little box with a crank and two wires that ended in little handles. When you turned the crank, electricity shot down the wires. Grandpa would get us all to stand in a circle and hold hands. He'd give the handles to the two people on the ends and say, "Hang on, kids." And then he would crank the thing as fast as he could and send electricity through our bodies. Some would call it an electrical shock; Grandpa said it "tingled."

"Don't let go or you're a sissy," he'd say.

We wanted to be strong. We needed to be brave. So we hung on for dear life. Of course, it hurt. But Grandpa had such a smile on his face that we knew it made him happy. The crank-o-matic became known as the Sissy Machine, and we asked Grandpa to pull it out at any family gathering where we felt the need to get shocked.

Grandpa died when I was sixteen, and Grandma started dividing up his stuff. "Steven," she said, "none of the other grandkids like this as much as you do." And she gave me the Sissy Machine.

That's how I decided to close my traveling Halloween show that day.

"Kids, get in a big circle and hold hands because the ghosts are coming. Just close your eyes. And . . . don't let go, or you're a sissy."

They joined hands, and I cranked it up Grandpa-style, and they screamed like crazy, and that was the end of the show. I packed up all the stuff on the cart, wheeled it to the next room, and kicked in the door. Lather. Rinse. Repeat.

My science show moved from classroom to classroom with a trail of smoke following behind. I did the show over and over, wall to wall, all day. Every hallway at Willow Creek Elementary hung with gummy bear smoke. We quickly discovered the smoke alarms didn't work. The entire school smelled like a campfire. What a day.

Renée got home before I did that afternoon. She was still in the insurance business at the time. I walked in, and she looked at me like I had just crash-landed in the yard.

"What happened to you?"

I told her the whole thing, and she paused because she's a reflective person. Then she said, "Isn't it amazing that today those kids told you what you should be doing for the rest of your life?"

✳

The next day was pretty special. Kids were high-fiving me in the hallways, a custodian threatened my life, and best of all, I was told that the principal, the great Dr. Deena Tarleton, wanted to see me at the end of the school day. I was sure there was going to be a ceremony in honor of the best Halloween in the history of Willow Creek, possibly the state of Colorado. I was going to get a classroom. There would be a marching band, cookies, handshakes, and a plaque.

I walked into Dr. Tarleton's office. The only other person there was a man I didn't know.

"Steve, this is Mr. McPherson."

"Hello," I said. "Steve Spangler."

"He's Gabby's dad," said Dr. Tarleton.

"Third-grade Gabby?" I said.

He nodded.

"I love third-grade Gabby."

"Thank you," he said. "I just wanted to ask you about a couple of things that Gabby shared with us last night. I was asking Dr. Tarleton about it, and she suggested I talk directly with you."

That's your principal throwing you under the bus, but I didn't know it back then.

"Am I right to understand," he said, reading from some notes he had scribbled on a yellow legal pad, "that you detonated an explosive in a classroom in front of a group of children?"

Long pause.

"*Detonate* is such a strong word, Mr. McPherson."

"We heard about the barfing pumpkin," he continued. "We don't really understand that, but Gabby said you made the carpet change color."

My marching band vanished.

"I heard about the fire and the gummy bear," he said.

I considered how much I could make as a hotel clerk or coffee server. He continued with several other questions before he got to the big one.

"But the part we really don't understand is that you may have had the kids circle up and hold hands while you cranked a machine and sent electricity through their bodies."

You know the feeling you get when all the blood drains from your face and passing out is mere moments away?

Dr. Tarleton spoke for the first time. "Chuck," she said. "Tell the kid why you're here."

Gabby's dad looked up from his notes.

"I know everything you did," he said. "Because Gabby told us. Last night is the first time ever her mother and I didn't have to ask what she did in school that day. The story started before we sat down to eat for dinner. As we set the table, the monologue continued. Through the mac and cheese and the hotdog, she talked and talked and talked. I know everything you said, every joke you told, even the cracking-cup prank she played on us. We were practically done with dinner, and she hadn't touched anything. Finally, Gabby said to us, 'So, Mom and Dad, that's what I did in school today—BAM!' She punctuated the *BAM* part with two fingers pointing right at us."

I didn't know what to say, so I didn't say anything. I was thinking about whether Renée knew a lawyer.

Mr. McPherson continued. "'Gabby, what did you think about all that?' I asked her. She looked into my eyes and said, through her first bite of hot dog, 'Best day ever!'"

The walls were sort of moving around me at this point.

"'Did you tell Mr. Spangler it was the best day ever?' I asked. 'No. I hugged him. He knows.'"

I remembered that hug.

"You have Gabby's undivided attention," said Mr. McPherson. "She would do absolutely anything for you right now. I came here today to let you know that. You have her attention. Do something with it."

It was the best piece of advice a parent has ever given me. Create an experience, leave room for connection—then do something with it. Don't waste these precious moments. They don't come around often. When they do, seize the moment.

If It Gets to the Dinner Table

That was many years ago, but I've never forgotten the impact and influence that day had on me as a teacher, as an employee, as a dad . . . If I'd known back then what I know now, I would have spotted Gabby's obvious excitement and keyed in on her sense of transformational engagement. This was her Van Gogh moment (well, I'm sure one of many, but this one she shared with me).

I should have taken just a second out of my time with the class to go over to her and say something like, "I noticed you're having a great time today. If you really like this kind of thing, you should sign up for the after-school science club in the spring. Then, you might want to ask your mom and dad about going to that hands-on science camp at the rec center. Then, you should think about taking more science classes when you get to high school. Now, go make another batch of slime to take home . . . you earned it."

But I didn't know to do that. Not yet, anyway.

As Dr. Tarleton and I walked out of her office that day, she had a few questions for the guy who nearly passed out while being interrogated.

"Steve, what did we learn today?"

"I learned never to do that pumpkin thing!" I quickly responded.

"No, that's not what we learned. Think on a deeper level. What did we *learn* today?"

"To cover the floor in a protective coa—"

"NO, Spangler. Think like a teacher. *What did we learn today?*"

198

"I don't know!" I didn't. I had no idea what she wanted.

"If it gets to the dinner table, you win," she said.

✳

I'll pause here to let that sink in.

Activities don't get to the dinner table; experiences do.

Transactions don't get to the dinner table; transformation does.

> **Activities don't get to the dinner table;**
> **experiences do.**
> **Transactions don't get to the dinner**
> **table; transformation does.**

My first principal had just handed me a core memory—you know, a deeply significant and emotionally charged memory that becomes foundational to one's identity. It's the kind of gift that shapes how a person views the world and themselves.

"If what you shared with your students is more than a cute little activity or something out of the standard teacher playbook," she said, "they will internalize it, make it their own, and they won't wait to share it with anyone who will listen."

I can hear Dr. Tarleton's voice as I put her words on paper:

Remember, activities are transactional—part of an *if you do this, you get to do that* kind of transaction. "If you sit here quietly and organize all the stuff in the box into the classification groups we're studying, you get to have ten more minutes at recess." That's what I mean by transactional. But when you create an experience, you give your students the gift of making the experience their own by injecting part of themselves into it.

Experiences are transformational—they have the ability to change the way your students see, feel, think, and react.

It wasn't until many years later that I realized my principal had probably orchestrated this experience for me. I have no doubt Gabby's dad said something in passing to Dr. Tarleton. Knowing her style of leadership after all these years, I wouldn't put it past her to have asked Mr. McPherson to step into her office while she sent word for me to join her for a little chat.

Create an experience, allow for connection, and cultivate engagement. Well played, Dr. Tarleton. You changed my life. If that's the power of transformational experiences, I'm in—hook, line, and sinker.

The Lesson

- One act of encouragement can rewire someone's sense of worth and potential.
- People don't always remember content, but they remember how you made them feel.
- Every student, colleague, or employee is one moment away from shifting how they see themselves.
- As leaders, we have the power to change someone's internal narrative by simply believing in them out loud.
- If the story gets to the dinner table, you win. That's when you know the experience mattered enough for someone to carry it home, retell it, and make it part of their personal narrative.

PART 3

PURPOSE: CULTIVATING ENGAGEMENT

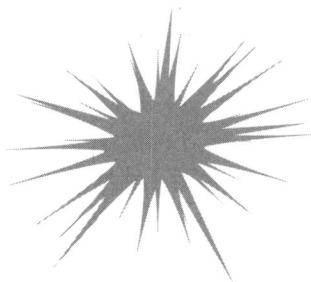

CHAPTER 25

BETTER BE GOOD

THE WEEK AFTER MY CONVERSATION WITH GABBY'S DAD, I WAS BACK on the A/V cart, roaming the Willow Creek halls—a man without a classroom, a real teaching nomad, but *very* happy I didn't have to find a lawyer or a new job.

The squeaky wheel was a messenger of joy as I rolled into Gabby's third-grade class. With Thanksgiving just around the corner, it was the perfect time to teach the kids how to whip the tablecloth out from under all those plates and glasses. Newton's Laws of Motion, right?

"Gabby, I met your dad," I said.

"I know."

"You told him about the fire? I said not to mention the fire."

"I did," she said, sassily, "and you didn't get fired."

The narcissist in me couldn't wait any longer, so I asked what I had come to ask.

"So, Gabby . . . thank you for all the things you told your mom and dad at the dinner table. Thinking back on everything you did that day, what was the *best day ever* part?"

"The gummy bears," Gabby said without a second of hesitation.

"No, Gabby, not the fire. Let's forget the flaming gummy bears. Of all the other things that day, what was the *best day ever* part?"

"When we built the things with the gummy bears and the toothpicks and the marshmallows."

"Honey," I said, "we didn't build anything with gummy bears, marshmallows, and toothpicks."

"I know *you* didn't," she said. "But after you left, Mrs. Ridgley got the stuff from her closet, and we made things. We built a bridge thing out of marshmallows and toothpicks and some gummy bears. That was so cool. Our team won."

"Building things was the best part of the day?" I said, crestfallen.

"Yep."

I'm sure Gabby noticed the long pause. My brain was going a thousand miles a minute. The *best day ever* part wasn't me.

The hard truth is that you may not be around to benefit from the engagement you cultivated. Sometimes you tee it up, and somebody else comes in and smacks it down the fairway. It could be a teacher three years down the road. It could be a boss at the job after the next job. When you're dealing with children, there's a high probability that you will never hear about it.

Recognizing that there's something bigger than your influence, that it's not all on you, should be liberating. I thought about Gabby's *best day ever*, and I realized that sometimes it's just my job to prime the pump. But it's also my job to be deliberate about it.

The last thing Mr. McPherson said to me before I started hyperventilating was, "You've got Gabby looking forward to science. You're going to have her again next week. It had better be good."

He was right. I'm a science teacher. If I can get a kid ready to engage in science, it's my job to look into her eyes and say all the things I should have said to Gabby, but even more: "You like this? There's a job waiting for you. They haven't even invented it yet. It's called STEM. You're going to be happier than you could ever imagine. You get to wonder and discover and explore. You get to ask questions.

You'll have a career you love, not a job you'll regret. All you have to do is sign on the dotted line. Just say yes and go for it."

That was hard for me to learn how to do, because I'm not a salesperson. But I figured it out. When they connect, they connect hard. That's why you must be ready to help them take it to the next level. We do such a good job of getting their attention that sometimes we forget to sell it at the end. Better be good.

✴

I was bitten by the teaching bug because of my high school chemistry teacher, a guy by the name of Doug Hodous. I took his chemistry class when I was a junior. No one was ever late for Mr. Hodous's class because the excitement started before the bell ever rang. He was always prepping for his opening demonstration. Demonstrations are different from experiments because they're more like attention-getters or conversation-starters to get the ball rolling. Things would fizz, pop, catch fire, explode, and the next thing you knew, you were caught up in Hodous's little adventure. I quickly learned the burn marks on his lab coat were real. Kids who sat in the front row often put out fires on their own desks.

Hodous was the teacher you always wanted to have, and I consider myself one of the lucky ones to have had him. People just wanted to be in the room with this guy.

It took me a while to figure out his secret: He made you feel good as a person first and foremost, and then he taught you chemistry. It should come as little surprise that I would do anything possible just to be around him. I approached him at the beginning of my senior year with an idea for a science outreach program as my senior project. I convinced him to let me leave school, drive (his car!) to the local elementary schools in Littleton, and put on a little science show—blow stuff up, explain why it happened, and leave a stain.

"I will get little kids so excited about chemistry that they will be lined up to take your class," I promised. Trust me, he didn't need help filling his classes. I guess that was my marketing brain kicking into action.

Hodous went for it, but he knew I couldn't do it alone. Volatile chemicals don't ignite themselves, so Mr. Hodous pulled me aside while I was in the planning stages.

"You see the new girl in Advanced Placement Chemistry? The blonde?" said Mr. Hodous.

"Of course," I said.

"She might make a pretty good partner for your traveling science show."

"That's the captain of the varsity soccer team, vice president of the National Honor Society, future homecoming royalty. I don't think she'd—"

"I command you. Ask her if she wants to do the show with you."

Hodous was a super funny guy, but I didn't know him that way when I was eighteen years old. I mustered up the courage and asked the beautiful and wickedly smart blonde if she wanted to help me do science experiments for kids at elementary schools once a week. Much to my astonishment, she said yes. Her name was Renée.

Renée and I snuck (OK, *drove*) Mr. Hodous's car out of the faculty parking lot and put on our little science show for fourth- and fifth-grade classes all over the school district. We only got busted when we showed up on the front page of the *Littleton Independent* as an "innovative hands-on science program" touring Littleton Public Schools. You see, Doug Hodous never got permission from his principal or anyone else to allow a few of his students to leave school and do a traveling science show—and certainly not in his car. Now I understand why he used to say, "It's easier to beg forgiveness than to ask permission."

At one time, I thought I was going to be a high school chemistry teacher. I could have been, and that would have been great. But that wasn't the point for Doug Hodous. He saw that he had connected with a student who was ready to fully engage, and he provided that student with opportunities and resources. In other words, he crafted the experience but left enough room to make me feel like it was my own. There was no pressure. The ideas for my show were taken directly from the demonstrations he did at the beginning of his classes. He was the perfect role model. No pressure—just space and support. One thing leads to another. That's engagement.

**No pressure—just space and support.
One thing leads to another. That's engagement.**

As for the Renée thing, that wasn't a lucky coincidence. Hodous knew exactly what he was doing.

When I got my first teaching job at Willow Creek Elementary, Doug Hodous was the first person I went to see. He loaded me up with even more demonstrations, complete with extra glassware, gizmos, funny props, and pages of jokes and one-liners. He set out to help me be the best teacher possible.

When engagement escalates to the next level, the personal connections grow deeper and the experiences become more meaningful. Doug and his wife, Jan, attended our wedding, attended birthday parties for all three of our boys, and became wonderful family friends. When he retired from teaching in the mid-'90s, I offered him a job as codirector of the National Hands-on Science Institute in Denver. We taught together for twenty-two years until he retired for the second time in 2019.

It might start with a *best day ever* or a pretty girl or a borrowed car, but engagement is a slower burn. A kid can have five best days ever in the same lunch period. Don't get too hung up on that. Recognize it as an acknowledgment that a connection has been made through a shared experience; that's when you spring into action. That's when you'd better be good. Engagement is not a given in the current day and age. True engagement is a gift from a student to a teacher, from an employee to a manager, from a customer to a salesperson. That's why it's essential for us to talk about how to recognize and steward that gift.

> **True engagement is a gift from a student to a teacher, from an employee to a manager, from a customer to a salesperson.**

Engagement is the endgame behind what we do as leaders, teachers, parents, and friends. It is what we want for those we lead, teach, and love.

As a leader, I create an experience; when it works, I feel a mutual connection; that's when I have to *do something with it*, as Gabby's dad told me.

But engagement can unfold over decades . . . or it can lie dormant for half a lifetime. It might also blossom in private. If Gabby's dad hadn't set me straight, I would have spent the rest of that school year thinking the real win from my Halloween spectacle was mine, not Gabby's. At best, I would have recognized the connection and left it at that.

Engagement is something we pour ourselves into and cultivate with no hope of personal gain. As teachers and leaders, our ambition is on behalf of others. In that generosity, engagement shares a lot with experience and connection; it is, however, the trickiest to talk about because it can be so devilish to pin down and because it relies so deeply on forces outside of us, the ringmasters.

But fear not. We are engagement obsessives here in Spanglerland, and we have found that the best practice is to identify engagement where it manifests itself and then track it in reverse.

The Lesson

- Sometimes the real *best day ever* isn't yours. You may spark the engagement, but someone else delivers the magic—and that's OK. That's the job.
- "If it gets to the dinner table, you win." Engagement that lives on beyond the moment is the gold standard. It means you created something worth retelling.
- You don't always get to close the deal—but you'd better be ready when the moment strikes. When a student is hooked, your next move matters most.
- Great mentors don't just share content—they hand over the keys and create space. That's where ownership (and transformation) begins.
- Engagement isn't a transaction—it's a gift. And when someone offers it, your job is to steward it, amplify it, and turn it into something lasting.
- Engagement doesn't always pay off in the moment—and it might not be your moment. Sometimes you spark the energy and someone else delivers the impact.
- Students (and colleagues) remember how you made them feel—and what you made possible. Sometimes the *best day ever* has your fingerprints all over it, even if your name's not on it.

CHAPTER 26

MENTOS & DIET COKE

YOU HAVE TRAVELED BACK IN TIME. YOU ARE IN A WORLD IN WHICH the Internet is just a curiosity on the news sometimes. The # symbol means *pound*. You don't know what @ means. Telephones are connected to walls in buildings. A/V carts squeak down the halls of your elementary schools. You've never heard of Mentos because it is a seldom-seen, quirky candy from the Netherlands, and you definitely, *definitely* don't know what happens when Mentos are dropped into Diet Coke.

In the '90s, I worked as an adjunct professor in the chemistry department at Regis University, offering professional development courses for teachers during the summer months. One of the science experiments we did during the workshops was to put a stack of Wintergreen Lifesavers on a pipe cleaner and hang them in the air pocket inside a two-liter bottle of Diet Coke. When it was time to trigger the reaction, we let the pipe cleaner holding the Lifesavers fall into the soda. The resulting soda geyser shot up twenty feet in the air. Pure magic.

Here's the science: Carbon dioxide gas wants to come out of a solution. It's like a genie, eager for release. When Wintergreen Lifesavers fall into soda, all the carbon dioxide in the soda runs to the little rough parts on the outside of the Lifesavers. These rough parts are called nucleation points. The nucleation points are a perfect place for the carbon dioxide to get a foothold and make their escape. If you put coral sand in there, the same thing would happen. You may have seen people salt their beer. It's a weird thing, but it starts to fizz a little bit. Same thing. No matter how you do it, the carbon dioxide shoots up into the air. Then the soda genie grants you three wishes.

The exploding soda geyser quickly became a favorite on the Spangler Science tour. It was the perfect finale for a school presentation, and teachers seemed to like it just as much as the kids. I was booked to speak at a big teacher conference in Dallas—a real stage in a huge auditorium. Just one bottle of Diet Coke and a roll of Wintergreen Lifesavers wouldn't be enough. So we set the stage for eight audience volunteers, each armed with a bottle of Diet Coke, Wintergreen Lifesavers, safety glasses, a stylish plastic poncho, music, the whole nine yards.

Unbeknownst to me, the people at Lifesavers had made a change. Wintergreen Lifesavers didn't come in rolls anymore; they came in green sacks that you bought at the grocery store. Inside the bags, they were individually wrapped. No problem . . . except that Lifesavers had also changed the size by two millimeters. Now the little mints were too big to fit into a bottle. In other words, I didn't test it ahead of time.

I got everybody lined up and poncho'd, we did a countdown to drop the Lifesavers in, and the teachers all looked at me like I'd pranked them.

"These don't fit. Funny joke, Spangler."

It was not a funny joke. We ended up trying to smash them on the table, but a Wintergreen Lifesaver is pretty hearty. It was a disaster. One of my top 5 all-time embarrassing moments on stage, and that's a competitive field.

Word spread in the professional mess-maker community that Wintergreen Lifesavers didn't work anymore for the soda volcano. Then a chemistry teacher from Naperville, Illinois, named Lee Marek let me in on a little secret.

"You know what?" he said. "Mentos. I think Mentos would work."

"What's a Mentos?"

"It's this candy from the Netherlands or Italy or something. You should try them. They're heavier. Good nucleation sites. I think they would work."

Things could still be hard to find at the turn of the millennium, Mentos among them. But I got my hands on a few rolls of Mentos in a specialty candy shop and tested them. Mentos don't have a hole, so the pipe cleaner was out, but if you put them in a tube or something to drop a handful in together, they worked great. Really great. Problem solved. The mess machine was back on the road.

I did it on TV three or four times. People seemed to like it, but that was about it. There were probably a few kids in the Denver area who tried it at home if they knew where they could get their hands on some Mentos, but I never heard about it.

Fast-forward to September 2005. I was in the backyard at 9NEWS in Denver, one of the largest NBC affiliates in the country. It was an outdoor set they used for segments that needed a little extra room. Ward Lucas was retired by then, but I was doing weekly science segments with one of my favorite people on the planet, Kim Christiansen, a regional anchor who was the epitome of style and class. A local treasure.

On this particular day, Kim was dressed in a gorgeous St. John's outfit with perfect hair and makeup to boot. Kim and I had a few two-liters ready and a bunch of Mentos in some tube contraptions I had rigged to drop half a dozen Mentos into a bottle at once. Thinking back on it now, I should have brought her a poncho . . . but could I really cover up *that* outfit? Please!

"Now, listen," I said. "Those Mentos are going to fall fast. When they do, all the bubbles inside are going to rush to the candy like kids when the piñata breaks. We might see a little eruption. If you don't stand back, there could be a problem. Are you ready?"

"I'm ready."

She was not ready.

"OK. Three, two, one, drop in the Mentos!"

Kim had a Diet Coke, and I had a Diet Pepsi. I guess in all the lead-up, she didn't really understand what I meant by *stand back*. The second the Mentos touched the liquid, the enormous soda geyser erupted. Bubbling soda went absolutely everywhere, including all over her thousand-dollar outfit.

"That's awesome!" I yelled into the camera. The camera guy also hadn't heeded my warning to stand back.

Kim's face and hair were covered in diet soda, but she smelled minty fresh. I offered my apology, but I wasn't sorry at all. We had just made great TV, as the people in the business say. Did I mention that this was *live* television? The producer in my earpiece yelled, "Do it again!" I did . . . two more times. We tried root beer, and then we tried some sort of Sprite thing. By the end, Kim Christiansen, Denver's classiest, coolest, nicest news anchor, was absolutely drenched in a mixture of Diet Coke and liquified Mentos. While I stayed outside to clean up the mess, Kim went back into the studio to jump behind the anchor desk to finish out the four o'clock show. The crew hopelessly tried to fix her hair and makeup. Her clothes were in need of dry cleaning, to say the least. She was a mess.

But the station loved it, and so did our television viewing audience. The phones went nuts. Emails started pouring in. Half of the audience wanted to know where to buy Mentos; the other half was mad at me for subjecting their local sweetheart to such shenanigans. During the five o'clock broadcast, every time they came back from commercial, Kim's co-anchor said, "Well, Kim looks a little funny right now because of Steve Spangler." And then they showed a clip. They ran the clip on every newscast that evening—the six o'clock, the nine o'clock, and the ten o'clock. I got more airtime than you could ever imagine.

Server Crash

The term *blog* was relatively new at this time. I had just launched my own blog a few months before all of this happened, and it seemed like a pretty good thing to blog about. The post read, "News Anchor Soaked When Science Experiment Goes Awry." It included a link to the Mentos Diet Coke eruption video on the 9NEWS website. That was a Tuesday. Just in case my friends happened to miss my blog post, I sent the link out to the two hundred thousand teachers on our email list. That's right: *two hundred thousand*. Within hours of sending out the video link, our highly curious teachers from all over the country crashed the 9NEWS website and the whole Gannett server.

I was summoned to the news director's office.

"Listen, these little on-air hijinks are way out of line," he said. Imagine him chewing a cigar and having just gotten back from closing an orphanage. "People who don't even live in Colorado are streaming this segment. What were you thinking? It costs us money every time they watch it."

He was right. There was no free streaming at the time. Gannett paid for every second that was streamed from their site.

"Never do that again," he said.

"Yes, sir, message received," I said, scurrying out of his office.

My next stop was an editing bay, where I pulled down the video from the 9NEWS server and uploaded it onto an upstart video website someone had told me about. The site was just three months old at the time. It was called YouTube. Fun fact: When we posted this in September 2005, YouTube was attracting about thirty thousand visitors per day. By the time YouTube officially launched in December 2005, it was serving more than two million. Today, YouTube serves up over two billion video views daily.

I uploaded the Mentos geyser video to YouTube and started throwing the link out. It changed my life.

✳

For years and years, we had been telling kids the same thing: Don't try this at home. Don't try anything at home. Don't try anything dangerous. Science is dangerous. Blah blah blah. The Mentos experiment was the opposite: *Not only should you try this at home, but you should upload a video of yourself doing it.* That's why it took off. It wasn't the giant erupting soda geyser (OK, that helped). It was the *doing* that followed. It was the engagement.

Somebody scraped the 9NEWS video from my original post and posted it on their own account. They got 1.7 million views. Back in

2005, you were viral if you had twenty thousand views in a day; 1.7 million views was earthshaking. Instead of posting a copy of my video, eager creators were running out to the store to buy their own geyser-making supplies and posting their own. All of a sudden, everybody was doing it, whether or not they wanted to post it online.

In the flash of a soda bubble, the Mentos Diet Coke thing became pop culture. You might think I became famous for this, but I didn't (yet). A comedy duo called EepyBird rolled onto the scene after seeing my video and turned my single bottle and a roll of Mentos version into a symphony of exploding soda geysers set to music. They became famous . . . for a year or two . . . but my goal was longer term—to turn a simple activity into an unforgettable experience.

I wrote an entire science curriculum teachers could use in class to illustrate the difference between a physical and a chemical reaction and the science of carbonation. I thought about the reaction day and night.

Prior to our YouTube success, I made multiple attempts to reach anyone at the candy company that made Mentos. The company, Perfetti Van Melle, was based out of the Netherlands, but they had a US division in Cincinnati. For some reason, I couldn't get anyone's attention . . . until the original video took off. In January 2006, I got an invitation to meet with their national brand manager. It felt like that meeting in the principal's office all over again.

I guess I should have asked more questions before jumping on a plane to Cincinnati. Was I in trouble for using their product without getting permission? Was a lawsuit just around the corner? I couldn't imagine they just wanted to spend a few minutes chatting. Well, that's indeed what happened. The meeting turned into more of a performance and presentation for a group of six executives who peppered me with questions about my work in education, how long I had worked in television, and that "toy" I had invented.

Finally, the national brand manager cut to the chase.

"I think we would all like to know what you want," he said.

What did I want? How about a Get Out of Jail Free card, if I'm in trouble? But something told me this was different. I got the impression they thought I had pulled this little media stunt to get their attention. Maybe subconsciously that was true, but I needed to come up with an answer in the next three seconds.

"I'm glad you asked," I said. "As you can see, I'm excited about the launch of my new science toy. I'm calling it the Geyser Tube. I think the product would sell best if a roll of your Mentos was included on the blister card packaging. As you might know, the toy market is a cutthroat business, and I'm just a science teacher with an entrepreneurial spirit. The likelihood of a big toy company coming in here and stealing my idea is pretty high, so I'd like to ask you to give my toy company, Be Amazing Toys, exclusive rights to include Mentos with our Geyser Tube toys and science kits."

"Let me see if I understand what you're saying," one of the executives said as he clasped his hands. "You are looking for exclusive North American distribution rights on Mentos for the education market?"

I could feel a small bead of sweat starting to form on my upper lip.

"Yes, sir, I believe that would be the better way to put it."

There was maybe a five-second pause as the Perfetti Van Melle executives looked at each other.

"What else do you want?" another person asked.

"I'd like to ask for one hundred thousand rolls of Mentos."

"For what?" she asked. I could feel everyone hanging on my next words.

"I think what we've come up with here is the next vinegar and baking soda volcano. It's going to be the new gold standard for kids as they think about science fair projects for generations to come. As you saw in my presentation, I've already written ready-to-use lessons for teachers to share in their classrooms. All they need is a bottle of soda and a roll of Mentos that I'll give them as a gift from you."

Deep breath. I'm not really sure where all of that came from, but in a nutshell, that's what I said. I explained that I was scheduled to speak at over seventy-five teacher conferences and events over the next twelve months; this would be a great opportunity for me to put their product and my lessons in the hands of teachers who will share the experiment with millions of kids all over the country. (Remember, YouTube was still in its infancy. There was no social media to speak of. This was a guerrilla marketing concept coming from a nerdy science teacher.)

Before they had a chance to respond, I reached into my briefcase and pulled out a clear plastic test tube. The open end was sealed with a cap like the one you would find on a two-liter bottle of soda. Sealed inside the test tube was a single roll of Mentos with instructions for how to use the test tube to help launch the perfect soda geyser.

Here's the kicker . . . the "test tube" was actually a two-liter soda bottle before it was inflated. All soda bottles start out as one of these test tube–looking containers called a "preform," which is heated and expanded into a bottle with high-pressure air. I had figured this out while playing around in the workshop at our science kit manufacturing company in Denver. I was looking for a way to easily pour Mentos into a bottle of soda before running for cover. These test tubes solved the problem and doubled as a wonderful way to distribute a hundred thousand rolls of Mentos to teachers from coast to coast. This would serve as a makeshift way to get my idea on the market and in the hands of teachers until my actual Geyser Tube toy—designed to drop five Mentos into the bottle at once—was ready for production.

As you probably guessed by now, the Mentos people said yes, and the rest is history.

Renée and I spent a significant chunk of our retirement savings to prototype and eventually patent the Geyser Tube. When we had it perfected, it would launch soda suds thirty feet in the air. The Geyser Tube toy made its debut at the New York Toy Fair in 2007 and has been selling in toy stores big and small, brick-and-mortar and online, ever since. That toy put our company (Be Amazing Toys) on the map, and our three boys got to go to college. You can still buy a Spangler Geyser Tube Toy today on Amazon or wherever you buy toys that leave Diet Coke stains on your ceiling.

The Geyser Tube became the tool of choice for science fair enthusiasts, backyard scientists, and content creators, who spent countless hours trying to come up with the best combination of Mentos and soda to produce the biggest geyser. Countless videos were posted comparing brands of soda in hopes of finding the Holy Grail of soda. From the perspective of a science teacher, this was pure gold. Students came out of the woodwork to engage in their own, self-directed science projects where they used the scientific method to put soda brands to the test. Does generic soda work as well as brand-name soda? Does temperature play a role in how high the soda shoots into the air? Does altitude make a difference? Did Steve Spangler's geyser work so well because he's in the mile-high city of Denver? What would happen if we tried it on the International Space Station? Engagement soared because science enthusiasts everywhere of all ages connected to the premise of my initial experience with a news anchor in Denver.

To understate: Engagement was off the charts. People were posting their own Mentos & Diet Coke videos at a record clip. There were pranksters, soda-launching competitions, people trying to come up with better explanations, people coming up with fake explanations, even fake news stories about people drinking Diet Coke and eating Mentos only to explode seconds later, like some twisted reboot of the old Pop Rocks and Coke myth.

Thousands, maybe millions, of people chose to engage on their own terms, and all because something we posted on YouTube encouraged them to play along and showed them how. Many of these people felt so connected to the phenomenon that they created their own YouTube accounts to post their own videos. And newly minted YouTubers couldn't wait to comment on other people's videos, telling them how to make their geysers better or to point out what they did wrong. It was real-life organic engagement of a scale and speed that had been impossible before the Internet age.

Why Diet Coke?

Good question. The easiest and best answer has to do with clean-up. Regular soda reacts just as well, but the clean-up is a sticky mess. Because diet sodas don't contain sugar, the aftermath is easier to wipe away.

In the original television segment we did at the news station in Denver, Kim Christiansen used Diet Coke and I used Diet Pepsi so as not to play favorites with our advertisers. But you'll notice the phenomenon was never called the Diet Pepsi and Mentos geyser. That's because all the focus was on Kim's bottle. She's the fabulously dressed one who got drenched on live television. When the Associated Press picked up the story from the 9NEWS website, they only mentioned Diet Coke and Mentos.

Of course, this infuriated the marketing geniuses at Pepsi. They spent considerable time and money trying to hijack this pop culture phenomenon with offers to supply teachers and YouTubers with free bottles of Diet Pepsi for their large-scale events. But the jury of public opinion had already cast its verdict. The phenomenon would go down in history as the thing that happens when you drop Mentos into a bottle of Diet Coke.

＊

OK, that's a fun story and one of my favorite memories, but unless you take a time machine back to the 1990s to upload your own Diet Coke and Mentos video to YouTube the day before I did, what does all this have to do with you? What lesson can you take away and apply to your work?

That depends on your angle.

Mentos wouldn't call me back until YouTube and the public response made me unignorable. Only when they saw the proof of concept did they choose to engage. But I only got onto YouTube because I broke Gannett's website. So, for the business folk:

- Be visible.
- Be the bad boy.
- Get there first. I know (I *know*) there is a certain amount of fate involved in this one. But being up for anything, saying yes to risk—What if I sent this link to the entire email list? What if I published this on YouTube, whatever that is? What if I invested our kids' college fund in designing a Mentos tube?—is the only way to hit the jackpot. Maybe that's the real lesson ...
- Be risky and frisky. Don't let fear of embarrassment prevent you from taking some chances.

Don't let fear of embarrassment prevent you from taking some chances.

At the end of the day (even today), Perfetti Van Melle thinks what we did was the dumbest thing anyone has ever done with one of their products, but they cannot deny the pop culture phenomenon it created, and they knew at the time that it behooved them to be part of it. They engaged because thousands (now millions) of people created their own Mentos experience, many of whom posted their creative ideas on YouTube and other social media. The license agreement I signed with Perfetti Van Melle to include a roll of Mentos with our dropper device is still in effect, as it has been since 2006, and our Geyser Tube toys and kits remain top sellers for the Steve Spangler Science brand in stores and online worldwide.

For those in the engagement game on a smaller scale, the lessons are similar.

- A party needs partiers. Whether you're teaching a science class or giving a keynote presentation, sometimes you have to win over the majority of the room before the other half will play. One hundred percent participation is tough, but the path to 95 percent runs straight through 50 percent.
- Don't be jealous. Basement-dwellers scraped *my* video and stole *my* views. EepyBird homed in on *my* Mentos idea and got a ton more. Did I waste my time litigating? No. I got busy making my tube while they created a market for it.
- When they forget about you and start creating on their own, you are witnessing genuine engagement. I've said it over and over in these pages: Your ego has no place in the engagement game.

✳

While I would never say all of this made me famous at the time, there is something kind of fun about getting to share the story in newspapers, trade journals, marketing textbooks, and a few thousand online articles. I'm honored to get to say I was one of the first YouTubers during those Wild West days of the Internet who landed a deal as an influencer and launched an entire line of educational toys and hands-on science kits.

We set a Guinness World Record for the most Mentos dropped into Diet Coke bottles (at the time). Then came a question about it on the television game show *Who Wants to Be a Millionaire?*—and that's when the phenomenon really snowballed. Suddenly we were hearing stories about TSA agents stopping travelers carrying Mentos and Diet Coke, or people joking about what would happen if a Mentos truck crashed into a Diet Coke truck. It just kept growing.

In 2007, I was even named a contender for *TIME* magazine's Top 100 Most Influential People. I beat out Howard Stern in the published rankings. He hated that.

The Mentos thing opened a lot of doors for me. It also taught me a ton about what engagement can look like in the internet age. That video got a lot of views, so we made six hundred more videos. At the time, views were everything. If you got a million views, the YouTube people behind the big curtain would look at you.

But that was still magic show thinking. *Look at me! Look at me! Look at me!* That's not engagement. YouTube already knew that. Little did I know at the time that YouTube was looking at our comments more than our view count. A few years later, that would put us back in bed with them in a big way.

The Lesson

- Spectacle can be a gateway to curiosity. Big, bold moments grab attention, and attention is the entry point for deeper learning and connection.
- People remember what surprises them. A well-timed eruption—especially one that's messy and unexpected—can create a story they'll retell for years.
- Engagement multiplies when people stop watching and start doing. The real success of the Mentos geyser came from the millions who recreated it, made it better, and turned it into a shared experience.
- Being visible matters—but being first, being bold, and being willing to take a risk matter more. The soda geyser moment worked because it was unpolished, unpredictable, and unforgettable.
- Let go of ego. You may not get the credit, but if people take your idea and run with it, you've won. That's the purest form of engagement.

CHAPTER 27

WHAT IF WE JUST *ASK THEM* TO ENGAGE?: SICK SCIENCE

IT DIDN'T TAKE LONG TO FIGURE OUT THE FORMULA FOR YOUTUBE: Find a cool experiment. Fire up the camera. Teach people the science behind the gee-whiz. Smile a lot. Don't say bad words. Post it to the YouTube channel.

In those early days, our metric for success in terms of engagement was the number of views we were getting. If a video really struck a chord, we would get lots of views, and that meant people liked us, right? That's what this was all about—validation from complete strangers around the world. Looking back on it now, the early years of YouTube were like the Wild West for content creators like me. We really didn't know what we were doing; we were all just posting content and seeing who liked it.

Something about this laissez-faire attitude bothered me. As a teacher and a performer (some would say a combination of a scientist, a magician, and P. T. Barnum), I thrived on feedback from my students and my audience. Unlike television, YouTube provided a way for people to connect through the commenting feature. If you liked a video, you gave it a thumbs-up. If you had a YouTube account, you could comment on other people's videos. The troublesome part for me was in the quality of the comments. Most were short and ... sweet?

"Coolio. The egg exploded"

"U R funnie and I like it"

"Dude, the 80s called and they want their shirt back."

Maybe reading comments wasn't the right thing to do, especially if you didn't have thick skin.

What I liked about YouTube was that it allowed me to go beyond the four walls of my classroom to reach anyone with access to a computer. I started looking at this opportunity through the eyes of a teacher: Instead of haphazardly posting my favorite experiments, what if I organized the content into a quasi-curriculum with the hopes of viewers coming back week after week for new stuff.

It was a revelation. It felt like coming home. I pulled together our small but hardworking video team, and we committed to creating a weekly web series that featured short experiments using easy-to-find materials at home. That was the key: simple materials that made the experiments easy to re-create. We had the concept, but we needed a name.

One day I was working with a class of fourth graders making tornadoes in a soda bottle when one of the boys yelled out, "Man, that's *sick*!"

Sick? I thought. *What does that mean?*

So I asked him.

"Oh, you're old," the kid said with a little chuckle in his voice. "Sick means cool, slammin'. You know, *awesome*."

I paused to ponder.

"So ... today we've been doing some *sick science*, right?" I asked.

I could tell by the smiles on their faces I had found it. *SICK Science* (written this way because that's how the kids wrote it in their notebooks) was not just a great name for a web series; it was a constant reminder that the experiments we posted needed to provoke that *sick* response.

SICK

The problem was that I couldn't be at the office to film these weekly experiments for our newly created web series. Carly had done a great job booking me all over the place, so I was on the road constantly. I asked the two guys on our video team to come up with something.

A couple of weeks later, when I got back from who-knows-where, the video guys came to Carly and me and said, "I think we got it." They put us in the screening room, turned off the lights, and played us their idea.

It was a guy's torso (with a way flatter tummy than mine) in a plain blue T-shirt against a blown-out white background. Apple did blown-out white backgrounds, and we always thought that was a very clean look. A materials list appeared onscreen in time to an annoying little song with glockenspiel and woodblock. Without saying a word, torso guy put colored water on a plate, set a candle in the middle, lit the candle, and covered it with a glass. The water rose into the glass, the candle went out, and a sentence appeared onscreen: "Share your conclusion on how you think this happens by leaving a comment below."

That was it. One minute on the dot. The lights in the screening room came back on.

"That sucks for so many different reasons," I said. "OK, I like your creativity not showing the guy's face. Intriguing. But first, don't you think *I* need to be in the video? Second, you didn't really teach anything because there was no one—me—talking . . . explaining why the water rises in the inverted cylinder. And that music, whose idea was that? People will hate the music."

(Carly, bless her, says I wasn't really this mean or narcissistic at the screening, but that's how I remember it, to my eternal shame. I'm sure it will all come out in therapy.)

The video guys were steps ahead of me, as always.

"Steve, you should take a look at this."

They had posted it already. We had over 5,500 views and 850 comments in the first hour. A normal video for us might get 1,000-plus views but only 6 to 10 comments on average . . . definitely not anything close to 850.

"Oxygen's not being used up because, according to the laws of conservation of mass, the oxygen cannot disappear. Rather, it combines with hydrocarbons from the candle to form water vapor, carbon dioxide . . . "

Who is this person? Why are they schooling in the YouTube comments? People were arguing with one another.

"The fire warmed the air inside, causing it to expand and forcing it out from beneath the glass . . . "

If I had asked a high school student to write at this level as a homework assignment, I would be thrilled with the effort, no matter how asinine the explanation they tried to drop on me. And they were doing this for fun on YouTube.

The secret was that last little sentence: "Share your conclusion on how you think this happens by leaving a comment below."

The link for the show description sent you to our website, which told you exactly why the water rises. If they clicked the link, they got the answer. They didn't click the link. They didn't want *my* answer. They wanted to contribute *their* answer. In other words, they wanted to engage at a higher level. Create an experience (check), leave room for connection (check), cultivate engagement (check), glockenspiel (ding!).

Lather, rinse, repeat. We made 225 *SICK Science* videos over five years and licensed them to school districts, media outlets, and publishers around the globe.

Renée's office was right next to the editing bays. She walked by one day and said, "I'll pay for the licensing agreement for another piece of music. Pick *any* other piece of music." So we recorded three episodes with different music. The audience let us have it in the comments. We had to bring back the glockenspiel. It was part of the experience, just like the nameless torso guy.

✳

Here's one of the quickest experiments we did: Eat a bag of potato chips and flatten the bag. Put the bag in a microwave. (Don't do this at your home. Do it at a friend's home.) Heat for a couple of seconds, watch the lightning flash, and see what you get. It will be a miniature version of the bag. It preserves the letters and everything. All we had to do was put that out there. No explanation at all. "Share your conclusion . . . " People commented and commented and commented.

"It happened because the magnetron radiates the energy in the form of wavelengths . . . "

"Thermo-ionic emissions . . . "

"Knowing how it works doesn't make it any less fun. :-)"

Who are these people? Who cares? They're engaged.

"Aluminum does not change in any way to boron . . . "

Who talked about boron? We didn't say anything about boron. We dug through hundreds of comments to find whoever brought boron into the conversation. People were totally engaged with one another. We were forgotten.

We set up the parameters. We framed the experience with significance. Then they were on their own.

"Oh my goodness. It works, but it smells horrible."

"It's one inch long by two centimeters wide." (This is why we have a math problem in the United States.)

"Now it shows how many chips you actually get."

Regenerative Engagement

I learned a lot from *SICK Science*. First and foremost: It's not all about Steve. I should have learned that from Gabby, but it's a hard lesson for a guy like me. It took decades and an international audience of anonymous boron enthusiasts to school me.

From a business standpoint, I learned that if you allow your customers the space to engage, they will. But only if you get the heck out of the way.

A lot of businesses are afraid to do this. They're afraid "boron guy" is going to write, "This sweater from L. L. Bean sucks." So what? It's your job or the job of someone on your team to slide into the comments and say, "Hey, I'm really sorry you didn't like the sweater. What didn't you like about it?" When you engage them, they feel connected. People will choose that over an automated system every time because when you form that connection, that's an experience in itself. The cycle has doubled back and become regenerative.

As I write this book in 2025, we have almost 4.5 million followers across all our social media and over 5 billion views between all the videos. We have not counted the comments. (Side note: It's probably not a good idea for creators to read their comments unless they want to go to therapy three times a week. People can be brutal.)

Carly gets business inquiries weekly from companies that want to learn how we got millions of eyes on our online content.

"You're a nerdy science guy. We're selling cool gadgets. What gives?"

They are typically displeased with our answer. It's all about momentum. In purely scientific terms, momentum equals mass times velocity. Stick with me. Let's start with velocity.

Velocity is defined as the speed of an object in a specific direction, meaning it tells you how fast something is moving *and* the way it's going. Essentially, it's "speed with direction." In business terms, I like to think of it as not just doing something as fast as you can but making sure you have a purpose for doing it. We knew we had to crank out a new video every week, and the videos had to feature an eye-catching experiment viewers could do at home using easy-to-find materials. That's speed with direction or *purpose*.

You know what mass is. In a business context, mass represents our body of work.

Momentum = Mass x Velocity

Producing just one video quickly with purpose has less momentum than fifty videos with purpose. See how it works? Momentum increases as mass (body of work) increases—assuming velocity isn't zero.

> ## Producing just one video quickly with purpose has less momentum than fifty videos with purpose.

This was why most companies didn't want to hear our answers to their questions about engagement and connecting with an audience. There's no silver bullet other than hard work and a commitment to the vision.

If your eyes glazed over two paragraphs ago, here's a simpler way of saying it: The momentum ramped up when we stepped out of the way and invited folks to write (pretty much) whatever they wanted. Engagement was the direction element in our velocity.

60 Percent Disengagement

A couple of years after I told our video guys that the *SICK Science* videos sucked without me and then they showed me why they didn't, someone high up at Google (which owns YouTube) approached us. I was floating in the ocean on a Mediterranean cruise with my family when I received a text from Carly.

Sorry to bother you but someone from YouTube/Google really wants to get ahold of you. They keep calling and emailing.

I thought it was a scam, but Carly's follow-up text proved otherwise.

FedEx showed up today with a thirty-eight-page nondisclosure agreement. I scanned it and sent it to our attorney. He says it's the real deal.

It felt a little like one of those oh-no moments from my past, only this time, someone wanted to talk to us, and we would be sworn to secrecy. What a great way to get my undivided attention. Fully engaged.

They were kind enough to put the meeting on hold until I got home.

"We like your science videos," they said. "We've binged your television appearances. OK, there are too many to watch everything, but we've got a pretty good idea of what you can do. And we've watched your *SICK Science* series. As manager of the EDU division, I know whenever my team is watching one of your videos because of the annoying glockenspiel music. Suffice it to say, we know a lot about you. That's why we think you would be perfect for a little test we want to conduct."

At the time, the average viewer on the planet watched YouTube for two minutes and twenty-one seconds a day. YouTube wanted that number to be much higher, say twenty minutes, because that would change the viewing landscape. YouTube would go from the quick, how-to-fix-something website to a platform where people would go to consume longer-form content. So YouTube approached a hundred successful creators and distributed a hundred million dollars between them. Not a million each, sadly (tragically), but we were given a budget to do exactly what the education team at YouTube wanted.

We had to step away from the one- to two-minute videos and enter the land of long-form content. That's when we came up with *The Spangler Effect*. The show featured cool experiments you could do at home (mostly) to amaze friends and family and to hopefully get all parties hooked on science. Since making science fun had been my passion for many years, *The Spangler Effect* made sense.

YouTube's experiment was this: As soon as you lose 60 percent of your audience, we're going to consider your audience to be disengaged. We want to measure how long you can keep them. We're not going to do anything. No advertising. We're not pumping you up in the algorithm or doing anything special behind the scenes to send traffic your way. We just want to measure your organic audience. When does your organic, natural audience become actively disengaged? We're going to arbitrarily say that's when you lose 60 percent of them. YouTube had no editorial content control (as long as we didn't do anything totally irresponsible, because we knew kids were watching).

The cubicle people at YouTube surprised us with some demographic intel. They shared data that showed most of the people watching Steve Spangler content were between the ages of 18–34 and 65 percent were female. All this time, we thought we were creating content for middle and high schoolers. We knew kids were watching, but we had no idea our demographic skewed so much older. We thought we knew our audience, and we didn't.

We took our YouTube bucks and hired six people at full-time salaries. We upgraded all our consumer-grade stuff to professional gear—lights, cameras, audio, and all the editing software and computers we needed. And we made the decision to bring in a heavy hitter to help us get this project off the ground. We needed someone with lots of experience . . . someone who knew how to engage an audience . . . someone from *The Ellen DeGeneres Show*. We had made friends with a number of producers from *Ellen*, and we were fortunate to have one of them agree to help us make the first few episodes great.

Every hit show needs a fancy opening intro with music, graphics, and explosions, right? Production value! YouTube money! So that's what we made. We produced the heck out of the first two shows. They really looked great. High impact. Great reach. All terms we had learned from those high-up television people.

The results were amazing, right? Not so much. In the first episode, we lost 60 percent of the audience in twenty-three seconds. Second episode, less than a minute. Failure on every level.

"This is good content," I said to our befuddled crew. "We're doing cool things. What's going on?"

Then, by accident, we tried a different open—something quick and simple. It was me looking directly into the camera, zoomed in real close.

"Hey, today I'm going to show you how to use the power of air pressure to crush a soda can like this." I turn an empty can over, put it in water, and *BAM!* it collapsed. "Coming up today on *The Spangler Effect.*"

The audience returned—and stayed—after 60 percent had bailed on the first show. We did the little sizzle thing after that (with an option to "skip intro"), and they still hung around.

The key was sticking to my own fifteen-second rule and then promising to show them how to do it. Whenever I made it easy and accessible, they connected. They engaged. We learned the same lessons I had been learning since I was five: Be quick, stay a step ahead, make it about them, not about you.

YouTube gave us the behind-the-scenes metrics so we could watch them unfold live. We could see when engagement started to drop, exactly when we lost the audience, to the millisecond.

As soon as I said, "I could do this with a gallon-size can," we lost them. Most people can't get their hands on a gallon-size can.

"Now we're going to go outside and crush a 55-gallon steel drum!"

We lost the rest of them. Engagement gone. They didn't want a magic show; they wanted to do something themselves. I could imagine thousands of viewers saying, "Hold on, Sparky, we're here to crush soda cans." The simpler I made the segments, the longer the audience stayed engaged. The experience wasn't due to the fun of watching me do it. The experience was viewers doing it *themselves*. *SICK Science* taught me (again) to be more interested than interesting. *The Spangler Effect* made sure we never forgot it.

Eyes and Ears

Among our new hires was a guy who sat at a laptop all day long, eight hours a day, and took out all the bad comments, all the pornography, all the political stuff, and then responded to the people who were actually engaged with meaningful comments. He made a plaque for his own door that read "Chief Engagement Officer," but that didn't change his salary. He responded to hundreds of comments a day. That engagement fueled the next people who found us.

"Wow, they listen. They're actually paying attention to us."

You can't just leave your YouTube channel open to what amounts to vandalism in the comments, but the businesses that are not successful on social media are the ones that are afraid to engage. They turn off comments altogether.

You can't just leave your YouTube channel open to what amounts to vandalism in the comments, but the businesses that are not successful on social media are the ones that are afraid to engage.

Whenever I address a business audience, I look into their power-vested hearts and say, "If you're turning off comments, fire your social media person right now."

This is as close to a hot tip as I have for those who are down in the trenches fighting for clicks. You're going to have to hire somebody who's intelligent and who can write to monitor your YouTube channel, Facebook, Instagram, and TikTok. Mine the gold that your customers are giving you. Turn your superfans into rockstars by featuring their comments. "Hug your haters," as my good friend and social media guru Jay Baer would say. Devote the time and energy to really connect with the people who are spending time engaging with you. Use every engagement opportunity to strengthen old connections (superfans) and forge new ones. When your followers, students, customers, coworkers, family members know that you're listening, they'll return to the scene of the crime to share more. They feel like they have the inside track with someone really important (that's you). Even the ornery ones! There are a lot of things to engage with today. If they're going to go engage with your brand, thank them in kind.

The Bad Boy Strikes Again

We posted a *SICK Science* video that illustrated how to make a paper airplane hover between two electric fans. First, you get two small fans. Then you fold a paper airplane. We teach you to make the right airplane—make sure the edges are creased, the wings are perfectly symmetrical . . . it's important. You really have to focus on that.

Once you've crafted your perfectly symmetrical airplane, take the two fans, point them toward each other at the same angle, and turn them both on. It's a wind tunnel effect. If you're careful, you can get your perfect airplane to hover between the fans. Magic.

"Share your conclusion on how you think this happens by leaving a comment below."

We got a lot of comments—more than usual. There were very detailed explanations as to how and why it worked using fancy formulas taking into account the coefficient of friction, air pressure at sea level, everything you could imagine. We got hundreds and hundreds of comments. We also got a lot of questions about why the experiment wasn't working at home.

We always released *SICK Science* videos on Wednesdays, because our behind-the-scenes intel revealed most of our subscribers watched our videos on Wednesday afternoon. That Wednesday happened to be April 1 . . . and you know by now that I love a good practical joke. That's right, our two fans and a paper airplane video was an April Fool's Day prank. The next week we posted a video showing the hidden fishing line that was holding up the airplane. Fishing line is invisible against a blown-out white background. April fool! We ended the reveal video with a new sentence: "Share your conclusion on why this is impossible by leaving a comment below."

And they did. People got mad. They told me where I could put the paper airplane and the two fans. We had to edit or delete hundreds of comments riddled with every curse word in the book. Some subscribers were so mad they found our number in my profile and called Carly.

"You WILL refund me for my fans."

"I boycott your channel forever."

"Hey Steve Spangler - $%@! YOU!"

Was *this* the engagement we wanted? No, not really. Did we do it again the next April? Yes . . . and for years to follow. It became a tradition, and our superfans LOVED it. Why? They felt like they were in on the joke. They were so connected with the creators at *SICK Science* that they had the inside scoop, and they couldn't wait to share their influence all over the internet. Our view count shot up big time right around April Fool's Day, and we think it was thanks to our fans sharing our videos with newbies who didn't know better.

If you watched network television around this time (2012), NBC was known for a popular series of public service announcements called *The More You Know*. I can still hear the jingle in my head. The fifteen-to-thirty-second spots highlighted important facts like, "Did you know playing with fire can burn down your house? Prevent unwanted fires by not playing with matches," blah, blah, blah. One of our video guys had the idea to produce our own series of public service announcements called *The Less You Know*. We produced graphics that looked just like the well-known commercials and even used similarly overly dramatic music. Now, all we had to do was come up with something to say.

"One out of ten people suffers from overexposure to dihydrogen monoxide. Left untreated, dangerously high levels of this chemical could even lead to death. Have your home checked today for leaks. Take action now!"

Can you see the tight headshot of the actor delivering the lines as the ominous music punctuates the seriousness of the message? We probably produced a dozen of these videos, each one about the dangers of dihydrogen monoxide. The only reason this joke works is that the vast majority of the audience was scientifically illiterate. *Dihydrogen monoxide* is just another way of saying two hydrogen atoms (dihydrogen) connected to an oxygen atom (monoxide). In other words, it's just water—good old H_2O. People either loved or hated the joke. It didn't matter, because *The Less You Know* campaign showed up everywhere.

You might be saying, "Steve, that's funny, but what's the point?" The point is to find an avenue to connect with your audience. When you see that something works (e.g., the fans and paper airplane prank), find a new way to do it again, and again, and again. Our April Fool's Day tradition became so popular with teachers that they used it to prank their students. Newspaper columnists shared it with their readers and pointed them to our video as proof . . . and then published the "aha" moment on April 2.

From a business perspective, everything that was "Steve Spangler" was connected to the Steve Spangler Science brand and our e-commerce store at SteveSpanglerScience.com. Stunts such as the floating paper airplanes and *The Less You Know* campaigns drove tremendous traffic to our site. We didn't have to slam viewers over the head with obnoxious banners or callouts to "Shop at SteveSpanglerScience.com!" Instead, we let people's natural curiosity drive them to discover more about this Steve Spangler guy . . . and they did. We saw a 15 percent increase in sales year over year during the *SICK Science* and *The Spangler Effect* years. Fostering engagement by connecting with our customers proved to be a very smart business growth strategy for this small but creative (some would say *scrappy*) educational toy company.

THE BRIGHT PRESENT OF SPANGLER SOCIAL MEDIA

Engagement isn't just for scientists, but a scientific mindset and a love for experimentation can be tremendous assets. According to available data, the average time viewers spend watching a TikTok vid/Instagram reel/YouTube short is around thirty seconds, with most users engaging with the content for a significant portion of the video's duration, especially if it's between fifty and sixty seconds long. In other words, shorter is better. We reverse engineered our content to match those trends, and it worked.[20]

Our goal in this new experiment was to grow a bigger audience. Luckily, we weren't the only ones with that goal.

TikTok called us in April 2020. They had the opposite request YouTube had issued in 2010. This time the digital wizards wanted shorter-form videos: under sixty seconds long.

If you recall what you were doing in April 2020, it probably involved way too much time indoors on a computer. Even with that caveat, we weren't prepared for the results of our TikTok challenge: We amassed one million followers in under sixty days and had five hundred million views in less than a year.

In the same vein, we launched Spangler Video Shorts in April 2022. The brief was simple: Take existing videos (if fact, videos we'd already posted!) and trim them down to the most engaging twenty to sixty seconds. That's it. Edit three videos per week and post them to YouTube, Instagram, TikTok, and Facebook. We committed to doing this from April to December 2023. We would then analyze the results.

The results were . . . astonishing. We gained 450,000 new YouTube subscribers in eight months. We were awarded our first Gold Play Button from YouTube (that's kind of a big deal if you're a content creator). Better still, we got over half a billion views and thousands and thousands of engaged comments during that time.

It had taken fifteen years to get our first million subscribers to our *SICK Science* channel. We doubled it to two million in less than eight months.

What if the wind changes direction again? It will! So what? We'll try something else with our much bigger audience. If you treat all of this like one big science experiment, it kind of makes sense in a strange way. The key, as with any experiment, is to create a hypothesis (set a goal), write a plan, conduct an experiment, gather data, analyze it, highlight your discoveries, formulate a new experiment, and do it again. Oh, and never forget to have a sense of fun and to never fear failure. Dust yourself off and do it again.

The Lesson

- Curiosity is one of the most effective tools in your engagement tool kit. If you spark a question, you've created an opening.
- Lowering the barrier to entry makes participation feel doable—and more people will join in if the first step is clear and easy.
- You don't need to design a masterpiece. You need to offer a simple, authentic invitation.
- Asking people to engage—directly and honestly—often works better than overengineering the experience.

CHAPTER 28

STEM CAMP

In March 2020, Miss America Camille Schrier was scheduled to come to one of our local elementary schools in Colorado. I worked for over twenty years as a consultant in that school district, in part to help organize a STEM Fest where students spent the entire day engaging in hands-on STEM challenges and learning about STEM-based careers. But our big surprise was Miss America appearing in person to perform the science experiment she'd done during the competition that won her the crown. The festivities were scheduled for a Friday. That Thursday, school was closed due to COVID-19. Disappointing, but no problem. We would just reschedule her to come back a few weeks later, when school reopened.

But days at home turned into weeks, and weeks turned into months. As a teacher who had used social media as a classroom before, the only thing I knew to do was open the laptop, go to Facebook, and say, "Hey, everybody! This stinks, but I've got a couple of activities I can show you, so if you want to join me on Facebook Live, it might be fun."

That first week, we had a couple hundred people. The next week, more than *forty-five thousand* tuned in.

Parents started coming out of the woodwork and hitting us up over Facebook. "What are we supposed to do with them all day?"

All the teachers were like, "It ain't easy, is it?"

"The kids go through material so quickly!"

"No kidding!"

Parents started asking us about STEM camp. I didn't run a STEM camp; this had nothing to do with me. Then, somebody in one of the comments said—with just a touch of snark—"Tough luck. Can't do STEM camp virtually."

That sounded like a dare.

✳

Years before, Renée and I had started a little company called Steve Spangler Science. Totally novel name. We ran that company for twenty-five years and stayed married the whole time.

In 2018, some wonderful people from Excelligence Learning Corporation—which owned much bigger education brands such as Really Good Stuff, Discount School Supply, and Frog Street—said they would like to buy Steve Spangler Science if we were interested in selling. Steve Spangler Science would merge with Really Good Stuff, and our brand would continue to grow and flourish. They said they would like to make it even better.

Steve Spangler Science was our baby, a company we had grown starting from a spare bedroom in our first house to a decent-size company, and I wasn't ready to sell. But truth be told, Renée was the CEO. She was responsible for the forty-seven people who worked at our headquarters in Englewood, Colorado. She ran the day-to-day operations while I was the face of the business, on the road speaking at conferences, writing books, and doing lots of television. After much consideration, I told the interested buyer that I wasn't quite ready to sell. Renée, on the other hand, said *Sold!*

As always, she was the smarter one. It was the hardest business decision we'd ever had to make. We said yes two years before the pandemic, and it was the best decision we could have ever made for us and the employees (who kept their jobs).

As a result, we were no longer in control of the more than three hundred and fifty products in the line, even though they had my name written all over them. (Think *very* hard before putting your given name on your business!)

When I was presented with the STEM camp dare, we approached Really Good Stuff and asked them if they would be willing to partner so we could run a virtual STEM camp using Steve Spangler Science materials. I wanted them to put stuff in a box and ship it to the kids who registered. I thought that was the secret. I wanted kids saying, "The box is here! The box is here!"

Really Good Stuff was all in. We announced a little STEM camp on Facebook, which included physical materials that would be mailed to participants. Carly said we'd take thirty spots—just register, pay, and receive a box in the mail. Before the end of that Facebook Live, the first camp was sold out. Carly suggested we add an afternoon session.

"Why not," I said. "I'll be tired, but that'll be fine."

The kids thought this was all for them. To be perfectly honest, a big part of it was for me. I accepted the dare partly because I didn't understand this medium called Zoom. Sure, I had thirty years of television time under my belt, but that's a one-way connection. Zoom is a two-way street; I can see them just like they can see me. That's what this was all about. If I was ever going to step foot in front of teachers again in any professional development capacity, I needed to log some considerable time in the Zoom cockpit.

Again at Carly's suggestion, we offered another camp the next week just to see who else might sign up. When all was said and done, we'd held five solid weeks of four camps a day: two in the morning, two in the afternoon—yes, *one hundred* total camps. Weekends were a time to regroup, sleep for twenty-four hours, and be ready for the next thirty Zoom squares filling my screen with little people who were stuck at home and just wanted to connect.

That might sound like a lot. Trust me, it *felt* like a lot! But we can't forget that classroom teachers do this day in and day out for a year or more. Say thank you to your teachers.

$$*$$

We saw kitchens transformed into STEM labs. We saw living rooms become learning centers. That's *best day ever* kind of stuff. That fuels my life. And I got a front-row seat to this amazing experience because I chose to engage.

I learned so much from this kind of engagement. The same parents who didn't want to be on the webcam on Monday were doing the projects *without their kids* on Thursday. Some kids weren't sure they wanted everybody else to see the inside of their houses, because they had seen the inside of everybody else's houses.

One kid showed up in the waiting room thirty minutes early to show me what she had invented the night before. Then every kid wanted to re-create her invention, and she was ready to teach. Sometimes, engagement is easy to spot.

One of our crew members would bring his dog, a black lab named Frank, to work with him. Frank wandered around the studio and occasionally made a cameo as he walked behind me. The kids loved Frank. Campers unmuted their mics just to yell, "Hi, Frank!" So one morning I said the next day would be bring-your-pet-to-STEM-camp day. It was just an off-the-cuff comment right before we signed off for the afternoon. The next day we had to make time for everyone to show off their pets. Over the next five weeks, we had chickens, goldfish, an iguana, frogs, a turtle, a snake, and lots of dogs and cats.

There was one little girl who hadn't talked for the first three days. She said nothing. Her engagement was zero, and it bothered me to the core. No matter what I tried (and I had thirty years of engagement strategies under my belt), I just could not reach her. She was trapped in the Zoom box, and I didn't know what to do. On the day we got to bring pets, she was the first one in the Zoom room. When Carly clicked "Start Meeting," this young lady couldn't wait to unmute. She did everything possible to get my attention. She talked and engaged for the rest of the hour, and then she stayed afterward to talk on Zoom. That was the connection she needed. She even showed me how she figured out her dog's nose was a conductor of electricity using the Energy Stick. Don't worry, the dog was perfectly safe . . . but water started rolling out of my eyes (must have been allergies). We connected, and it was all quite by accident.

We humanized the Zoom square by leaving enough room in the experience for her to connect in her own special way.

We humanized the Zoom square by leaving enough room in the experience for her to connect in her own special way. Over the years, I'm certain I've had students in class who didn't connect, and I incorrectly assumed that they just didn't get it or that maybe they didn't want to get it. Similarly, over the course of twenty-eight years of owning and operating Steve Spangler Science, I'm sure there were employees who just didn't work out for one reason or another—but maybe that reason was me and our leadership team. Maybe I didn't leave enough room in the experience for each of these people to connect in their own special way.

Don't get stuck on the dog thing . . . that was just one girl's medium to connect with me. She could see that I loved Frank and treated him with respect, and those were the cues she needed to be vulnerable enough to connect with me. That sweet kid gave me a *best day ever* moment I'll never forget.

✳

At the end of every day of STEM camp, the campers knew I would let them answer the question, "What was your *best day ever* memory from the time we spent together today?" Part of me was fishing for the runs, hits, and errors of the lesson; the other part of me wanted them to have the final word. Friday was our time for one last round-robin of *best day ever* memories.

When we came to one little girl, she said, "The *best day ever* was the virus."

"Oh, honey," I said, "the best day ever can't be the virus. That's why we're here."

She said, "If it hadn't been for the virus, Daddy never would've stayed home and done STEM camp with me."

That dad thought he was signing up for a silly STEM camp for his daughter, and he ended up sharing an unforgettable experience with her. The angel on my shoulder whispered into my ear, "Remember, it's not always about you . . . in fact, it rarely ever is."

Not sure why, but my allergies started acting up again.

✳

You can't control other people's circumstances, but you can recognize them. As a leader, your people's engagement must be fundamentally about them, even when you stand to benefit from it.

I got more out of COVID-19 STEM camp than those kids did, but that was only possible because of what we offered them. By meeting them where they were—stuck at home, unable to go out to buy supplies—we created an experience that invited connection during a difficult time for everyone. I'd never seen people so eager to engage.

So how does this translate beyond a pandemic or a virtual camp?

If you're a teacher, it might mean shifting the focus from delivering content to creating space for students to take the lead—letting them show what they know in a way that feels natural to them. Maybe it's project-based learning. Maybe it's giving them permission to teach the class for five minutes. It's about recognizing that connection happens when students feel like contributors, not just consumers.

If you're a business leader, maybe it's rethinking your next team meeting. Instead of marching through an agenda, start by asking what your team is proud of this week or what's been challenging. Build in space for people to show up as human beings, not just job titles. Sometimes the breakthrough doesn't come from the strategy deck—it comes from someone's story.

Creating space doesn't mean giving up structure. It means allowing people the freedom to find themselves in the experience. That's what builds trust. That's what drives engagement. It's not about grand gestures; it's about micro-moments of connection that authentically say, "I see you."

The Lesson

- When people live the learning, they own it. Real engagement happens when learners become part of the experience instead of just watching it.
- Virtual doesn't have to mean distant. With intentional design, online environments can still foster connection and creativity.
- Constraints (like a global pandemic) can become launchpads for innovation when you meet people where they are.
- Simple gestures—like bring-your-pet-to-STEM-camp day—can unlock the kind of emotional connection that transforms learning.
- Sometimes the most powerful engagement is about making room for people to connect in their own way, on their own terms.

CHAPTER 29

THE ENGAGEMENT BUSINESS WITH RENÉE SPANGLER

AFTER OUR HIGH SCHOOL CHEMISTRY TEACHER INTRODUCED US, Renée and I never really stopped doing science shows together in one form or another. One thing led to another and another and another. We just kept running electricity through children, blowing stuff up, and firing flaming gummy bears across classrooms, and then one day, someone handed us an Emmy for it. I get all the attention, but the organizational force, the business mind behind our empire of Mentos and rubber squids, has always been Renée, especially early on. Without her, most of my experiments would still be in the garage . . . and I'd be bankrupt.

All that said, it would be an enormously wasted opportunity if I didn't ask her to contribute at least one chapter to this book. So I'm going to sit this one out and let you hear from the boss.

The Shake-and-Bake Guy

As you already know, Steve and I met in high school. We attended the University of Colorado at Boulder together and both found a way to work our way through college to avoid that post-college debt thing. I worked weekends as a waitress, and Steve worked as a . . . *drumroll, please* . . . wedding DJ! By the time we got married in 1989, Steve had done nearly five hundred weddings, playing lots of Engelbert Humperdinck and Kool and the Gang. He continued to spin records (yes, there were still records in those days) even after we got married to bring in a little extra money. As his grandpa taught him, a little side hustle never hurt.

One night while packing up after a school dance, Steve fell while carrying a really heavy amplifier rack down a flight of stairs. He tore his ACL, had to have surgery, the whole thing. Steve hated being laid up. It gave him too much "thinking time," if I'm honest. But that thinking time ended up putting his future into focus.

Steve knew he wanted to be a teacher, but he also liked the idea of having a side job. Let's face it, Steve likes to perform. He loves being in front of an audience. That is his happy place.

Right before his ACL injury, he had taken an afternoon job running sound for a local high school that had hired a speaker from Minnesota. That was an easy gig—set up a few speakers and a microphone and sit back for the next hour while the speaker does his thing. I will never forget the look on Steve's face when he came home that day. It was a look of happiness mixed with astonishment, ambition, and a twist of apprehension.

"What happened to you today?" I asked. "Your brain is going a thousand miles a minute."

"I just saw the best speaker I've ever seen," Steve said with that look of astonishment taking over his face. "From the moment this guy took the microphone, he captivated two thousand high school students packed into the gym. These kids listened, they laughed, they loved him. When he wanted to turn the joke into a meaningful point, they got quiet, leaned in, and listened. You could hear a pin drop."

"How did he close?" I asked. I knew Steve's litmus test rested on how performers opened and closed.

"You wouldn't believe it. He did the 'Boomba-Hey' thing where every kid, every teacher, everyone was chanting 'boomba' and then 'hey' back and forth, louder and louder, until the whole place was on fire. Mic drop. I've never seen anything like it."

"What did you say his name was?" I asked.

"Mark Scharenbroich. Pronounced *Sharen-Brock*, kind of like Shake-and-Bake," Steve said. "I talked to him for just a minute at the end. He knows Earl Reum."

Dr. Earl Reum was one of Steve's all-time heroes. Steve could write an entire book on the impact and influence Earl had on his life. Earl taught junior high for years before becoming the director of student activities for Jefferson County Public Schools in Colorado. He helped establish the National Association of Student Councils and went on to found the National Association for Workshop Directors. He was a pioneer in the early days of educational television on PBS.

Earl knew Steve's dad because they were both magicians, and he used his magic to help illustrate points as a motivational speaker for students from coast to coast. Steve is who he is today in large part because of the influence Earl Reum had on him growing up. When Steve found out that Mark and Earl were good friends, that sealed the deal.

"I would give anything to one day be just a tenth as good as the guy I saw today," Steve said. "Seriously, he's everything I talked about in my graduation speech—the power of building connections." (Steve had been invited to be one of the speakers at our high school graduation. Big shock, I know.)

I heard about Mark Scharenbroich for the next ten years. This was pre-Internet (early '90s), so Steve had to track down VHS tapes of Mark to study his speaking style and maybe learn how he was so masterful at connecting with his audiences. Then, Steve found Mark's Emmy-winning film *The Greatest Days of Your Life… (so far)*. The film was so good that nearly every high school in the country showed it to their students during the 1980s. I tell you all of this because Mark Scharenbroich became Steve's gold standard—someone who inspired Steve to work harder than I've ever seen him work to hone his craft in the art of speaking.

Big leap forward in time: Steve and I really didn't get to know the great Mark Scharenbroich and his amazing wife, Susan, until we met in Washington, DC, for our first National Speakers Association conference. Steve actually got to sit next to his hero. That's when our friendship with the Scharenbroichs was born. Mark was so kind to Steve, mentoring him in the ways of the professional speaking business. Sue and I hit it off in a similar way—we each ran our husband's speaking business. We answered the phones, negotiated contracts, signed deals, and put our husbands out on the road to pursue their mutual love of connecting with audiences.

I was pregnant with twins in 2002. We knew we were having boys. One of them was going to be ornery (I could just tell), and we decided to name him Scott after Steve's grandfather, who was also a spitfire. One day late in the pregnancy, Steve came to me with a suggestion-question, as I like to call it.

"What if we named the other one Mark. I just like that name."

Steve teared up as he asked me the question. I knew how much this would mean to Steve and how special it would be for our Mark to meet the person who inspired his father to become the person he is today. Mark and Sue Scharenbroich had a front-row seat at Scott and Mark's graduation from St. John's University in 2024.

If I could give you one and *only* one piece of advice in business, teaching, or life, it might be to pursue the right mentor. Our trajectory without Mark and Sue is unimaginable.

Practice vs. Business

One day during the early days, when Steve was still doing traveling science shows, I told him I'd been doing some reading.

"We have a practice, not a business," I said. "Like a dentist has a practice. When the dentist fills your tooth, you pay them money. If they don't fill your tooth, they don't get any money. It's dependent upon people coming to you all the time. A business is where you make money even when you're not working. You could sell product."

Steve was booked to do a science show at a library about that time, and a local TV producer was there with her two kids. This was when television had to have educational content on Saturday mornings, which hadn't been a requirement before. The producer wanted to make a thirty-minute kids' show for Saturday mornings with Steve as the science guy doing three-to-five-minute slots. The show was called *News for Kids*. Steve started doing demos in three-minute spots.

People were contacting the show asking where they could buy the stuff he was using. That got me focused on the product thing. Why couldn't we produce sellable versions of the experiments? That discussion resulted in our first product, SQUIDY—although we never planned to have eighty thousand units on hand on day one. (Good one, Steve.) But we did feel there was a demand for the kind of science products Steve featured on the show . . . and it was time we got to selling if we ever wanted to fit a car into the garage.

The first orders were for teachers at conferences. We sold a few dozen here and there, but we needed much bigger orders. I wasn't sure how we'd ever sell eighty thousand units one or two at a time. We needed to wholesale these SQUIDY things to retail stores. Granted, we wouldn't make as much money per unit, but it was the only way we could sell hundreds at a time.

Soon, we had a wholesale sales rep who focused on getting us into toy stores across the country, and she made it rain. We would hold these little parties at our house where we persuaded (begged) my family to come over for dinner, and then we would assemble and package the products. On a good night, we could make five to eight hundred pieces ready to go out the door. My family had turned into our production line. That was a huge help because they worked for pizza and Pepsi. I would box up all the orders the next day and ship everything out. My sister and her future husband were our first full-time employees.

The sales rep we'd hired did such a good job getting our toys into stores that we outgrew the family pizza parties—too many orders and not enough space or people to help out. Steve had come up with about a dozen more products, and our resources were stretched thin.

That year, Steve and I planned a trip to Florida to meet our national sales rep face-to-face for the first time. We also booked tickets to Disney World. In the interim, the rep sold one of our gizmos to a gift store at Disney. I asked her which shop had it, but I didn't tell Steve anything. It was super fun to walk up to this little kiosk, this little cart, and see our product sitting there. That was a *best day ever* moment before I ever knew those existed.

✳

Aaaaaaand I'm back!

Over the years, Renée has taught me a *very* high percentage of the things I know that are worth knowing. What has she taught us here?

No one is too old or too young to be your mentor.

The Lesson

- No one is too old or too young to be your mentor. Our lives would be utterly different without Earl and Mark. Find your mentors and don't let them go.
- Say yes. When an unexpected opportunity (like a segment on a Saturday morning news show for kids) falls into your lap, take it and take care of it.
- Accept help where you can get it. Our early product business would have floundered without our family assembly line. Don't take advantage (and don't be stingy with the pizza) but let those who want to help do so.
- Don't be afraid to branch out, scale up, and dip your toes into new waters. Business is no place for impostor syndrome. If you're interested enough to engage, you belong!

CHAPTER 30

STEMTASTIC ADVENTURES

T HE BURROUGHS WELLCOME FUND IS A NORTH CAROLINA–BASED philanthropic organization whose grants support research and scientific education, specifically STEM engagement for K–12 students. The Burroughs Wellcome grant is a notoriously difficult one to get. Luckily, Dr. Amy Holcombe of High Point University is a grant-writing genius, and her idea was inspired.

Through the Burroughs Wellcome, HPU has brought Guilford County Schools, the Qubein Children's Museum, and *moi* into a partnership to engage 120 elementary students from backgrounds often underrepresented in STEM, plus thirty elementary public school teachers, in an experience we call *STEMtastic Adventures*. The purpose of STEMtastic Adventures is to motivate kids to pursue science exploration in STEM clubs, webinars with STEM professionals, DIY STEM activities in the home, and STEM camps. I was already on staff at HPU, and Dr. Holcombe knew I was keen to support this multiyear initiative.

The life forces of STEMtastic Adventures are *enthusiasm* and *community* both in its students and its teachers. Each student is paired with a teacher from their home school to receive over fifty hours of direct STEM learning; those teachers are paired with a wacky science guy from Colorado to give them some pointers on making science fun.

Dr. Dearing Blankmann began teaching at High Point University and working on the grant simultaneously.

"What I think the genius of this grant is," said Blankmann when I interviewed him during a Zoom call, "is that the professional development for the teachers and the STEM learning for the students go hand in hand. It's literally an experiential opportunity for the teachers to first engage in the PD [professional development] and then get to go and apply what they've learned in real time. All of this is based on Steve Spangler's professional development model from his time teaching at Regis University. We took those best practices and instructional strategies to the next level—because that's what we do here at High Point University."

I got to travel to High Point for some sessions and lunches with the first cohort of teachers, and then we had them all out to our Science in the Rockies session that summer. What a treat. Dr. Blankmann describes the event:

> The teachers insisted on two separate meetings to start planning their summer STEM camp, which was held the second week of July. You could see Steve's stamp on that entire camp. It was very, very evident. His antics, the leaf blower and the toilet paper, the Wow moment, the *best day ever* moment. . . . The teachers picked four scientific topics, one for each day, and then brought in everything they had done at Science in the Rockies. It was an absolute blast.
>
> It's one thing to see Steve do his "thing" on campus with our college students or back in Colorado at his summer STEM conference, but it takes on a whole new light when he trains

the teachers in our grant to do these demonstrations and experiments on their own. Steve's routine quickly morphs into something completely new as our teachers inject their own personalities, their own unique ways to connect and engage with our campers. Our president, Dr. Qubein, would say, "The impact and influence of this kind of personal instruction frames the experience with significance." I couldn't agree more.

The program is now entering its second STEMtastic cycle. According to the way the grant is written and the program designed, the first cohort of teachers was meant to pass the baton to two other teachers from their school. What we didn't anticipate was the strength of the created community and the sense of belonging that these teachers had built for themselves through our training workshops and summer institutes.

Well, guess what? The first cohort of teachers did not want to pass the baton. They *refused* to pass the baton. There was no separating them from one another. Colleagues had become a team and then a family. So they created their own community of practice adjacent to their successors in the official Burroughs Wellcome contingent. They meet monthly with Holcombe and Blankmann, and they are all launching their own after-school programs. They've also requested further professional development, which Dr. Holcombe somehow figured out how to fund.

The secret to student impact and engagement is engaged and ignited teachers.

The secret to student impact and engagement is engaged and ignited teachers. As Blankmann describes it, there's been a shift in how we approach science education over the last decade:

It used to be that [science education] was very didactic. It was all about telling the kids about science. It was all about learning the vocabulary. Scientific literacy meant being able to talk the talk, but the kids were never actually actively doing anything. That approach to science turned many—if not most of us—off. So, the scientists, engineers, and mathematicians in practice in the world worked closely with science educators to really rework and rethink our approach to science education. Belonging and community building occur from having these shared experiences of problem-solving together, from having *aha* moments. That's true whether you're a kid studying science or an adult studying how to teach science. This thing happens that brings everybody together, which is fundamentally, I believe, a big piece of that *best day ever*. That's part of what Steve does: these Wow moments that bring people together.

Another exciting part of STEMtastic Adventures is having the students talk with scientists in practice. They get to hear a little bit about the scientists' journeys and career pathways, but they also have a more casual Q&A space where they can ask all kinds of questions, which are often frankly marvelous.

Recently, a young lady who's getting her doctorate at Rutgers in the Ocean Sciences Department came out to HPU to meet with the kids. She's literally a storm chaser; she runs down hurricanes and studies how to anticipate and plan for them.

"One of the campers asked her how the change in the Gulf Stream impacted the hurricanes that we were having here in North Carolina," recalls Blankmann. "It's funny when it's coming out of the mouth of an eight-year-old. It's amazing how we can build on these interests when the opportunity is there, but it all starts with that Wow moment."

✳

That the teaching community is embracing the fun in education makes me smile, and not just because it's my bread and butter. In 1992, a grant proposal with the name *STEMtastic Adventures* wouldn't have made it past the slush pile. It's a new day for admitting that science is fun. That means a new day for engagement.

There is power in giving teachers permission to lose their minds with enthusiasm. There is power in giving students the opportunity to explore freely. I can't help but see Mr. Hodous, my high school chemistry teacher, in this. He didn't have Science in the Rockies or a grant to create a STEM camp, but his method was identical: Find the burning students and provide fuel for the fire. Admit that it's fun and lean into that.

You know who *does* have Science in the Rockies? We do. Let's talk about it in our next chapter so you can see how we prime teachers for engagement when we have them for three solid days.

The Lesson

- True engagement becomes scalable when you train others not just to replicate your strategies but to personalize them. Empowered teachers don't copy—they create.
- Community builds momentum. When teachers form their own microcultures around shared purpose and joy, they extend the life of your initiative far beyond your original design.

- Fun is not a distraction from learning—it's the delivery mechanism. When educators feel permission to lean into their own enthusiasm, students follow their lead.
- The spark of science engagement isn't reserved for kids. Grown-ups need "aha" moments too, especially when they're asked to pass that spark forward.
- If you want your work to matter beyond your reach, focus less on being the fire and more on being the match. The ultimate sign of impact is when your spark lights up someone else's fire—and they go on to ignite others.

CHAPTER 31

SCIENCE IN THE ROCKIES

MY PASSION IS INSPIRING TEACHERS TO FOLLOW THE PATH OF engagement in their classrooms, but for decades now I've also been one of those teachers who is trying to find the most creative experiences to make kids fall in love with science. If I can come up with experiences that allow them to connect and engage, they might fall in love with a future career.

Is the payoff decades down the road? Usually, yes.

Will I be dead before a lot of these kids have anything positive to tell me about the effects I had on them? Affirmative.

But at this point in my career (thirty-four years in), teachers do come to me at conferences and tell me they fell in love with science watching my videos when they were children.

"I'm a teacher now because of you," they say.

It makes a sappy guy tear up and cry, which I don't like to do at conferences, so maybe I get the flaming wallet out to distract us both while I pull myself together.

What I want to say is, "You watched my silly videos on YouTube, and you think it changed your life?"

But every single one of them can describe the exact video that they saw in *excruciating* detail.

"That was the one?" I want to say. "*That* one?!"

There's a reason teachers teach, and it's not just the health insurance. Teachers help kids find their passion. My passion is helping teachers find their passion for teaching. Or, in a lot of cases, rediscover it.

Carly has been working with teachers for decades, but since she was never a classroom teacher herself, she comes at it from a different angle. She explains:

> We see teacher burnout at all points in careers. It's not difficult to see when teachers have lost their passion, and it can happen for myriad reasons. They've often gotten caught up in bureaucratic minutiae, improper management, and poor leadership (that's the real killer of passion: poor leadership). It's tarnished why they started teaching in the beginning. One of the toughest things to see is a new teacher who hasn't found a way to connect, yet they are trying so desperately to engage.
>
> Then there are the teachers who are rounding the corner on twenty years in the profession, and you can tell they've lost their way. Something happened that caused them to forget why they wanted to be a teacher way back when.
>
> Although I was never a teacher, I've spent the last twenty years living, sleeping, and drinking the education business. I've been doing this long enough that I can spot a burnt-out teacher while they're standing in the registration line at one of Steve's events. What I want to do is grab their hand or give them a hug and tell them, "It's going to be alright. Steve's going to help you get reconnected . . . he'll help you rediscover why you got into the teaching profession in the first place." Of course, I can't do this because they would think I'm crazy, but I've seen it happen time and time again.

Whether it's a keynote presentation or a multiday workshop, participants will often line up after Steve's presentation to ask him to sign their event program or maybe one of his books. Some want to take a selfie, ask a question, or share a story. I can't tell you how many times I've been standing there when one of those burnt-out teachers I spotted earlier in the day thanks Steve for helping them rediscover their "why."

I remember a big, burly guy, twice Steve's size, who kept inching his way to the back of the line; he didn't want anyone else to see or hear him, I guess. When he finally got to Steve, he said (with tears in his eyes), "I've been teaching for twenty-three years, and I've been unhappy for about the last ten. I didn't want to come today, but my principal made me do it as part of my personal improvement plan. Today, you made me feel like a kid again. You helped me remember why I wanted to be a teacher all those years ago. I had totally forgotten about my middle school science teacher who made me fall in love with science. And to think I almost didn't come today."

I've also watched Steve grow and change over the years as these interactions have become more frequent. He used to do everything possible to redirect the attention to any place other than himself. But the guy who has spent years talking about the power of creating experiences that build capacity in others is himself learning how to connect and engage at a higher level. Those personal *best day ever* moments that people never see are the reasons why I love doing what I do.

If you have a respectful manager, you have a respectful office. If you have a happy teacher, you have a happy class. If you have *inspired* leadership, watch out. That's what we try to do at the workshops. Whether they realize it or not, they're coming to get reinspired to take a new breath. Nowhere are we more deliberate about that part of our mission than we are at Science in the Rockies.

✳

We have held the Science in the Rockies STEM conference every summer since the early 2000s. Two hundred teachers come from all over the world to spend three days with our team of presenters at a conference center in Lakewood, Colorado. The event attracts educators and administrators from early childhood, K–12, universities, and museums. From first-year teachers to thirty-year veterans, Science in the Rockies welcomes anyone who is in search of best practices and learning strategies to get children of all ages excited about STEM and STEM-based careers.

No spouses. No kids. No plus-ones. This is hardcore teacher stuff.

The three-day Science in the Rockies event is an intensified version of the five-hour professional development workshops we conduct for school districts. Some people refer to these workshops as "boot camps" because of our no-nonsense approach to learning. It's all hands-on, soup to nuts, and participants are busy the whole time. We encourage everyone to pack an empty suitcase, because we send them home with so many classroom supplies to use throughout the school year.

This is not your typical sit-and-watch lecture with a midmorning coffee break and a time to gather in "learning communities" to craft a mission statement. From the moment the teachers walk through the door, the energy is high, the visuals are eye-catching and fun, and participants quickly realize that they're in for a different kind of experience.

Carly and her team surprise everyone with a breakfast spread fit for a king (remember the Alaska cruise's first morning?), designed to give them nourishment for the next three hours of high-intensity learning. We kick off the morning with a few large-scale demonstrations: Leaf blowers turn into high-powered toilet paper launchers as we set the stage to learn how to harness the power of air pressure. For the next three hours, participants build contraptions that twist, turn, and fly through the air to illustrate fundamental scientific principles of air pressure. Eight-foot-long plastic bags· become the building blocks of life-sized structures that fill the ballroom. If TP'ing the ballroom wasn't enough, those same leaf blowers become Ping Pong ball launchers as teachers set up to do battle from opposite ends of the space. And that's just the morning session.

After lunch, participants roll up their sleeves and dive into the inquiry-based lesson they will be sharing with their students when they return to school. Each lesson turns into a diversified experience custom-tailored to students' age and ability. The combination of large-scale demonstrations in the morning and more personalized hands-on experiments in the afternoon makes for a truly unique professional development experience.

We do the same for days two and three. Surprise everyone with a few special guests and STEM experts and maybe a full-on potato gun fight in the back of the hotel (complete with an "I Survived Steve Spangler's Potato Gun Fight" T-shirt) . . . and that's a glimpse into what goes on at a Science in the Rockies conference.

The Sheraton Denver West Conference Center is terrific. On day one, I bring up and recognize the entire hotel staff. They're part of the event, and a lot of times, those people disappear from a group's consciousness. Our participants know they're part of our team. We all work together.

Carly sums up the event:

Science in the Rockies is transformational for teachers. People leave feeling different about their work. Our overriding mission has always been to make science fun. That's always been a big piece of it: allowing teachers to feel comfortable creating experiences that change the way kids think and see and feel. It helps kids fall in love with science, but it really helps them fall in love with *any* subject that they're into. When you understand the principle of *best day ever*, those experiences can be applied to anything. Nothing on our website says we help kids find their passions, but that really is what we do. We plant those seeds to inspire kids to engage and think differently.

Why Are We Talking About This?

If you're not a STEM teacher, you may be wondering what Science in the Rockies has to do with you. It has *everything* to do with you, because it has everything to do with building capacity in your people.

Engagement has levels, as we have discussed—from the card trick participant level to the Mars rover level. It also has multiple dimensions. Teachers aim to inspire engagement in the students they lead. We aim to inspire engagement in the teachers themselves.

Your goal as a leader is to inspire those you lead not just to engage but to inspire others in turn. When a principal or a school district sends STEM teachers to Science in the Rockies to learn from us, they are not doing it just because they think standardized test scores will go up. They're also doing it because developing their people into agents of engagement will make their schools better places.

Everything we have discussed, from experience to connection to engagement, has all been rooted in love and respect and service to those who follow you.

Everything we have discussed, from experience to connection to engagement, has all been rooted in love and respect and service to those who follow you. If you're a teacher, that's your students; if you're a principal, that's your teachers; if you're a manager, that's your reports. If your professional development budget is zero and you make three times what anyone on your staff makes, your budget is unbalanced.

Science in the Rockies is the best example I know of a deliberate investment that leads to the unquantifiable yet undeniable benefits of inspired engagement. You may not work with much slime (consider it!), but the same techniques we use at Science in the Rockies can energize the people you serve, no matter where your leadership takes you.

Boulder: The Novelty of Autonomy

People are used to being told what they're supposed to feel or do, especially at conferences. At Science in the Rockies, we take our teachers on an evening excursion to Boulder, Colorado, and turn them loose to explore on their own.

"What are we supposed to do here, Steve?"

"You are not supposed to do anything."

"Carly, help. What do you want us to do?"

"I want you to explore. We're jumping on the bus, driving to the iconic Pearl Street Mall in Boulder, and disembarking. Go where you want. If you want to get back on the bus, great. If you don't find your way back, here's the hotel address."

This seems like a freebie for us—bring them to the city and let them fend for themselves—but every time we do Science in the Rockies, the Boulder trip is one of the most profound experiences.

People have come to expect immediate satisfaction and immediate responses and immediate answers. The Wild West is stepping into a strange city without direction. That's become foreign to people.

As a kid, we went outside and just played outside. That's how I learned that the sun would go down over different horizons at different times depending on the season. Allowing people to feel that independence again, to be able to have a self-made experience in the midst of an organized, empowering weekend, takes them by surprise and opens up a part of their brain they had turned off.

We've primed them with experience, and now we give them room to choose connection.

We roll into Boulder in three nice buses. They talk. They have fun. Suddenly, they're drawn to one another and forming connections based on the shared experience they've been having. They become self-organizing. It's a very organic thing that happens.

One year, I drove my car behind the buses. I didn't want to take a seat. It was the biggest mistake in the world. Part of the experience was getting to see us offstage, as peers, which is what we are.

"Steve, where are you going to go?"

"I'm going down to explore Pearl Street. No plans. Just letting my curiosity lead me somewhere fun. You know, the TV show *Mork & Mindy* was set on Pearl Street."

There are restaurants everywhere, musicians, buskers, magicians, and the guy who can tell you where you're from if you tell him your zip code. It's a cool place to spend an evening. But the payoff is debriefing it the next day. I always come to the mic the same way the following morning.

"You were all like little kids last night. You all did the exploring on your own, and now you can't wait to tell everyone what you saw."

We couldn't believe it the first year we sent out post-conference evaluations:

"The best part of Science in the Rockies was the connections I made on the Boulder trip."

"Boulder gave me a chance to reflect on everything we learned and to meet new people I never would have talked to during the normal conference."

Our days at Science in the Rockies are pretty drilled down into STEM challenges and hands-on activities. They're packed. You're not there to socialize. But now you get to connect, not with me, the fearless leader, but with one another. We didn't know how important that was at first.

The big lesson for me: When you create an experience, you have to relinquish control.

✳

One year, a lady from Wilson, North Carolina, sat with me on the Boulder bus.

"Steve Spangler, can I sit with you?"

"Yeah, absolutely. I thought you'd never ask."

She sat down, and we took off for Boulder, but she didn't say anything. I started to worry because she was just looking out the window, a little forlorn.

"Well," I said, "how are things going?"

She started to cry.

"I didn't think I was supposed to come here," she said. "My husband was abusive. I took the kids, and we left the house two years ago. This year, my dad died. But before he died, he gave me the money to come here. I wasn't going to come. Then, at the last minute, I decided I would."

Obviously, that was a lot to take in. I'm sure I expressed my condolences and tried to stay open to her, but I have no idea what I said to that. I do know I told her how glad I was that she had come.

"I'm here," she said. "I don't know why I'm here, but this changed everything."

All she needed was somebody to listen to her story and say, "I'm so glad you're here. You're supposed to be here."

It's a science conference. I'm teaching Boyle's Law, not maharishi stuff. And yet, people keep having these incredible, profound, life-changing experiences while attending our science workshops.

A deliberate, safe space allows people to connect on a totally different, shockingly vulnerable level. It's like the friends you made at summer camp. Those are friends for life because even if you've shared a totally banal experience like paddling a canoe, you've done it in an environment that is so safe and free and open and encouraging of connection that you're linked forever. Those environments don't stop being effective and powerful when you grow up. They're just harder to come by.

Listen, I'm not trying to sell registrations here; Science in the Rockies isn't for software designers or bankers or mojito craftspeople. But whatever your profession, the people you lead—the people on the front lines of your business, the people who depend on you to get them the resources they need to do the job—need to be inspired to engage. It is essential that you, as a leader, learn to pursue shared experience, two-way connection, and inspired engagement. But sometimes you need to call for backup.

You want this for your people. Invest in their growth. They will pay you back many times over.

The Lesson

- Changing the setting changes the soul of the experience. When you remove people from their daily grind and immerse them in something different, you dismantle the habits and assumptions that often block engagement.
- The most lasting transformations don't come from the content itself, but from the emotional space we create for people to rediscover their purpose. Safe environments give permission to be curious, vulnerable, and authentic.
- When teachers are treated like VIPs—fed well, engaged deeply, and trusted to explore on their own—their energy returns, and with it, their capacity to spark engagement in others.
- Shared experiences outside the confines of traditional PD foster connection not just with the material but with one another. These off-script moments often yield the most powerful takeaways.
- Great leadership isn't always about steering. Sometimes the most impactful move is to step aside, relinquish control, and trust that what you've built will guide people toward the connection they need.

CHAPTER 32

ENGAGING YOUR WAY OUT OF TROUBLE

ONCE WE HAD A FEW *ELLEN* APPEARANCES UNDER OUR BELT AND figured out how a big TV talk show worked, we knew we had to always be working on something new. When the producers called, it was zero to sixty in a split second. Based on our experiences on the show, we concocted a formula that seemed to work: Show Ellen how to do something cool on a tabletop, then open the big stage doors to reveal the same experiment on a monstrous scale. That's where the phrase "anything worth doing is worth overdoing" came from.

We got a call from our main producer, who always started the conversation with, "Hey Steve, what are you working on?" I was ready for the phone call. The week prior, we had been trying to figure out how to do an explosion—because who doesn't like a good explosion on a daytime talk show? The catch was they wouldn't allow us to use traditional explosives or flammable liquids. When the producer called, we were ready.

The solution was liquid nitrogen. You might remember from your high school chemistry class that approximately 79 percent of the air we breathe is nitrogen. What could be safer than the air we breathe? I have a smile on my face even today as I share the story.

Scientists take the air we breathe, mostly nitrogen, and make it super cold to help separate it into different elements like nitrogen and oxygen using a special process called "fractional distillation." The super-cold nitrogen gas sinks to the bottom and becomes liquid. Ta-dah! You get liquid nitrogen that's -320°F. It's dangerous to handle unless you know what you're doing because it's possible to burn your skin if you touch it. No worries. I had been using liquid nitrogen for years.

As part of one of my previous appearances on the show, I demonstrated what happens when you fill a trash can with a few liters of liquid nitrogen and then dump in really hot water. An instant cloud shoots up fifteen to twenty feet in the air. That's because the hot water speeds up the process of the nitrogen transforming from a liquid to a gas. So much energy is released that it vaporizes the water to produce a beautiful, fluffy cloud. Magic.

Given what we'd just learned, it only made sense to see what might happen if you trap a small amount of liquid nitrogen in a two-liter soda bottle (my old friend!) and cap it off. For the lawyers and safety experts reading this, please note that I'm telling readers *never* to try this at home . . . or even at a friend's home (this time). There's a reason liquid nitrogen isn't something you can run down to the store and purchase. Nevertheless, I need you to stop thinking about trying it for yourself and focus on the rest of the story I'm telling.

Anyway, when liquid nitrogen changes from a liquid to a gas, it expands roughly 696 times in volume, meaning that the distance between its molecules increases dramatically. If the liquid nitrogen is trapped in a plastic soda bottle, that rapid expansion results in a big *kaboom*. Nice.

Out in our office parking lot, we made a little lab with buckets and trash cans. I was experimenting with putting the bottles in hot water, trying to get them to explode faster. They were going off one after another. *Kaboom*. Fantastic. When we knew we had something to go with, we started playing. What if we try this? What about this? Here's a thought . . . place a trash can *over* the smaller bucket holding the plastic bottle with the liquid nitrogen inside. Crackling noises were coming from the trash can as the plastic bottle slowly expanded. Wait for it . . . wait for it . . . the explosion turned the trash can into a rocket! For every action there's an equal and opposite reaction. We estimate the trash can shot up a hundred feet in the air. Watson, we have harnessed the power of the air we breathe!

We knew this would be too big to do inside the studio, but there was plenty of room outdoors at Warner Bros. where the segment would eventually be filmed.

Since practice makes perfect, we kept launching trash can rockets. Big ones, small ones, anything that remotely looked like a trash can went up into the air or suffered a terrible fate. We were having big, loud fun, over and over and over.

That's when police cars came flying into our parking lot with lights on and sirens blaring. We didn't get just the local police; these cars came in from three municipalities. They converged on us at the same time. It was a very well-orchestrated operation.

One of the guys on our demo team ran over to the police cars as the officers were getting out.

"Where are the shots coming from?" an officer asked.

"Uh, there are no shots. We're just practicing a science experiment. Do you know my boss, Steve Spangler?" he said. This is yet another example of getting thrown under the bus.

I told Carly to call our lawyer just in case I had to go to jail, and I told the video team who was recording our practice session to keep recording. It was my Beatles rooftop moment.

The police seemed relieved that we weren't firing weapons, but they were displeased that we were detonating bombs.

"Listen," I said, "it's for *The Ellen DeGeneres Show*." (As if that was going to get me out of this predicament.) "Can I just show you what it looks like? Actually, could I get your help? I'd love your opinion about this variation."

Did I need the police officers' takes on a variation? At the time, I would have said no, but it turned out a little differently.

All of a sudden, the police were interested, if still a little apprehensive. "I'm not sure we should be doing this," was written all over their faces. But they didn't stop us. We pulled the materials together and launched a few trash cans.

Our video team did their job, so the whole encounter was recorded.

After one or two more explosions, I turned to one of the officers and said, "What do you think?"

"Do that again, but try using hotter water to speed it up," he said.

Bingo. They were fully engaged in what we were doing, and that was because we had invited their participation and expertise, whether we needed it or not. You could feel the mood shift from "Steve's probably going to jail" to "Hey, the officers want to try to pour the liquid nitrogen." Pretty cool.

Before they left, the officers representing three districts invited us to huddle.

"If you boys want to practice your little science fair projects in the future, number one, call around so you don't panic the neighbors.

Number two, come and blow stuff up at any of our training centers. We'd love to help. We might even have some ideas for you."

This time, the bad boy should have asked for permission. I should have found somebody at the fire department and asked, "Would you help us create an experience that's even better than what I have planned? I need your expertise. I need your advice."

Quick aside: We took the officers from Denver up on their offer to practice our future "science tricks" at one of their training centers. In fact, we turned the whole thing into part of an episode on our nationally syndicated television series called *DIY Sci*. To this day, I still call these experts for their advice and tips as we come up with new ideas. They know their stuff.

It would have saved us some trouble if we had done that up front, but it's also a worthwhile defusing technique in a pinch. "Do you have two seconds to give me some advice?" It's like asking kids how to make mac and cheese. Make a connection, and engagement may follow. In this case, engagement turned into a greater understanding of what we were trying to do. It's like a preemptive thank-you. It might get you out of a pickle, and it might even get you some training you didn't know you needed.

The Lesson

- Engagement isn't just a strategy for teaching—it's a strategy for survival. When things go wrong, your best shot at recovery is creating a moment worth remembering for the right reasons.
- A well-timed *Wow!* moment doesn't erase mistakes, but it can reframe the story. When you shift the emotional energy in the room, you can shift the narrative too.
- People don't remember what went wrong—they remember how you made them feel during and after the chaos. Connection outlasts catastrophe.

- If you've built trust and credibility through engagement, people will give you the benefit of the doubt. That reservoir of goodwill can be the difference between disaster and a legendary comeback.
- Most importantly: Don't fake it. Genuine curiosity, honest acknowledgment, and real connection work better than any cover-up. If you mess up, engage forward—not backward.

CHAPTER 33

SPOTTER

W E'VE GOT STEVE SPANGLER AT THE 9NEWS STUDIO THIS MORNING. He's got a tub full of broken beer bottles, and he's told us to take off our shoes. You're not going to want to miss this."

The walking-on-broken-glass trick. I had been doing it for years at teacher conferences and our summer institutes. It's an old sideshow carnival stunt. People loved it because they couldn't believe they could walk on broken glass without destroying their feet. Soon, the cameras were rolling, and the news anchor was walking on broken glass while I followed along on my knees, hand outstretched if she needed it, explaining the distribution of weight and why she was able to come out unscathed. Spotter-scientist.

The scientific explanation is the same as the bed-of-nails trick: The weight of your body is spread across a larger surface area, so the individual nails—or in this case, shards of glass—don't puncture the skin. The crunching sound of the glass and the nervous look on the anchor's face make for fun TV and a chance to show off your pedicure.

The head of the station—the head-head, the Big Kahuna—sent someone to tell me she needed to see me afterward in her office. That usually means I'm in trouble. I went to her office as soon as we were done, meek in advance.

"Yes, ma'am?"

"Listen," she said. "All the Gannett managers will be in town next week. I need you to do the glass thing for them."

"Oh, well, thank you, that's ver—"

"But I need you to do it exactly the same way. With the knees."

"Ma'am?"

She looked at me like I was denser than she had thought. "The most powerful thing you did out there was you got down on one knee and held your hand out."

"Hmm?"

"You were her safety net. She walked on the glass, but you held your hand out and said, 'It's going to be OK. I'm here.'"

I'm sure the look on my face told her exactly how dense I was.

"I need to tell our managers that that's what I expect them to do for their reports. Our employees are going through tough times. It's tumultuous out there. Things are rough."

"For the managers?" I asked.

"That's what you were out there. You didn't have to walk on the glass."

"I have weird feet."

"As a leader," she continued, wisely, "I don't have to walk on much glass anymore. My job is to lend support and help to those who do. My role is to hold out my hand and tell our employees that they are going to be safe. That's the message my managers need to hear."

I scraped myself off the floor and walked to my car.

＊

I had gotten down on my knees because the anchor was nervous, and I was in charge of that moment; I didn't want her to freak out or chicken out or make a fool of herself on live TV, and I was probably the only one in the studio who knew without a doubt that her feet would come out unscathed. I thought I was teaching weight distribution. But the Big Kahuna engaged with that experience at a much (*much*) higher level. She connected because she recognized herself. Then she taught me something.

That's the cyclical nature of engagement. It has a living energy that circulates and comes back around to you, reprocessed, repurposed, reinterpreted, and more complex. This is why engagement *rules*. I love it.

＊

One more note about what the Big Kahuna saw. My spotter-scientist job was two minutes long; a manager's job is every day. It's easy to look down your nose after you've graduated beyond glass walking. That's a mistake. Once your shoes are back on, it's time to strap on the knee pads. Everyone needs a spotter. If there are people in your life who look to you for leadership, that spotter is *you*.

Everyone needs a spotter. If there are people in your life who look to you for leadership, that spotter is *you*.

The Lesson

- Quiet leadership can be just as powerful as what happens on stage.
- Trust is built when people know someone is there to catch them—even if they never fall.
- Not every role needs to be public to be essential. Support roles shape the outcome in critical ways.
- Sometimes presence matters more than words. Just knowing someone is watching out for you changes everything.

CHAPTER 34

SPREADSHEET JUNGLE:
THE QUEST FOR CORPORATE ENGAGEMENT

CARLY AND I WENT TO A JERSEY MIKE'S. WHO KNOWS WHAT CITY WE were in at the time.

If you're not familiar with the model, Jersey Mike's is a sandwich shop where you start by telling a teenager in a visor what kind of sandwich you would like, and then you follow them down the line as they top it as you direct. It requires a certain amount of back-and-forth that can be pleasant or unpleasant, depending on your teenager.

I requested the Number 7: turkey and provolone.

"That's great," said our teenager. She had a lip ring. "One of our most popular sammies."

"I get it all the time," I said.

"Hey," she said. "Do you have one second for me to ask you a question?"

There were other people in the line, and the energy around the condiments completely shifted as soon as she went off-script.

"Ask away," I said.

"Do you have any suggestions about what I could do this weekend?"

I looked at Carly. She shrugged.

"We don't live here," I said. "We should be asking you."

"Yeah, I feel you," she said. "Thing is, my boss is holding this contest for the employee who comes up with the most creative thing to do this weekend. He's gonna reward the winner by paying for them to do that thing. I'm just asking people as they come through the line."

"Hey, I've got one," said the guy behind Carly.

A lady elbowed in with her phone. "Have you ever seen this?"

"You ever tried the hot springs?" said another customer.

"What's the budget?" yelled someone through a mouthful of something, probably turkey and provolone.

I hadn't realized how full the place was, but the whole Jersey Mike's became a party game. We were going to take our sandwiches to go, but we stayed and hung out and talked with the locals about this teenager's contest submission for half an hour. Someone produced a yellow legal pad to write down all the suggestions.

A store manager at Jersey Mike's dresses different from the rest of the staff and is usually old enough to buy alcohol, so we recognized him right away when he came out to sweep up the house.

"Hey," I said to him. "That was brilliant what she did, getting everybody to talk like that."

"What did she do?"

I told him the whole story about the weekend and the manager and the contest.

"That's absolutely true," he said. "That contest is real."

"Seriously?"

"Oh yeah. I told everybody to come up with ideas."

"Are all the Jersey Mike's doing this?"

"Nah. This is our thing."

I thought the teenager was fudging to get everybody to talk. This was way better. The manager had created a culture, and his staff had bought in.

A few months later, Carly booked me to speak at a trade show sponsored by Jersey Mike's. The event was focused on employee retention and engagement. When I was being interviewed ahead of the event, I told the story to the Jersey Mike's coordinators.

"You have to tell that story in the keynote," they said. "Our CEO will love it."

"Are you sure?" I asked. "Is creating an experience in your core values as a company?"

"It will be now."

Faux Engagement

If you asked me to define my perfect audience, I would say five hundred educators crammed into an auditorium. There's just an energy in the air that's electric. All these years, I've been lucky because teachers are easy to hype. They recognize me as one of their own. They're effusive and feely, and group fun is their stock in trade. We give them Energy Sticks to take home, and you can practically see the lesson plans writing themselves beneath their early-graying hair.

As you know by now, most of my professional work has been in the field of education. A room full of excited teachers is my happy place. But over the years, the number of inquiries Carly receives from corporate event planners has increased drastically.

"I just got off the phone with the American Payroll Association," she said one day. "They're interested in having you keynote their meeting in the spring."

"Wait . . . *payroll* association?" I said, incredulous. "Accountants? Comptrollers? What do they want to know about teaching science?"

"They're interested in engagement. How did you get millions of people to watch your YouTube videos? How can they connect and engage more meaningfully with the people they serve?"

I didn't get it. I peppered Carly with more questions and more reasons why I probably wasn't the best choice for these people, but she wouldn't take no for an answer. She could already see the bigger picture.

"You've spent the better part of your career focused on human engagement. You understand what it takes to get a kid who couldn't care less about the effect of air pressure to want to become an air pressure aficionado. They want you to talk about the *best day ever* and what happens when you connect and engage through a shared experience."

As usual, Carly was right. In the end, the common denominator was our mutual interest in the art and science of engagement. They just saw it through a business lens. The language may be different, but the results are the same.

Business leaders want strategies that transform passive interactions into purpose-driven experiences—sparking curiosity, inspiring action, and driving real business results.

Business leaders want strategies that transform passive interactions into purpose-driven experiences—sparking curiosity, inspiring action, and driving real business results. Whether you're connecting with customers, motivating employees, or igniting creativity, engagement and building connections through customer experience are the key skills that set top performers apart. My job was to let go of my predetermined limitations and take all the knowledge I had gained through years of real-world experience to a new group of students (who just happened to lead Fortune 500 companies).

I'll let Carly explain:

A lot of potential corporate clients call me and say, "We want a speaker who can engage our audience. We want someone who can help them cut loose and play."

What they're really saying is, "We're tired of speakers who have five points and a poem or ninety-six PowerPoint slides followed by a round of Q&A."

For many reasons, I think the world of education has a real jump on corporate America, especially when it comes to understanding what motivates students (customers, in business terms) to go from passive learning (window shopping) to full-on interest in engaging a subject (making a purchase). As Steve will tell you, I (and a whole slew of his highly successful corporate speaker friends) had to convince him to share his educational insights with this new audience. However, all I really had to do was remind him of the importance of helping people from all walks of life understand the power of creating those *best day ever* moments for both children and adults.

Through interactive demonstrations and hands-on examples, Steve turns the audience into a living model of what's possible when experiences are positive, purposeful, and fun. This isn't just a keynote—it's a master class in engagement that redefines how they connect, lead, and inspire, leaving them with practical tools to create lasting, meaningful connections that elevate every experience they design.

The Jersey Mike's experience emboldened us (OK, me) to take on more corporate speaking engagements. Once we saw a big company keen to listen and willing to let their employees off the leash and embrace a surprise, it gave us hope.

I hope I don't get in trouble for saying this, but some corporate speakers peddle fake engagement with the old turn-and-talk trick.

Sometimes they sell placards that the audience can use to express an opinion—to "vote"—during the keynote. They can flip the placard this way or that way: green means I agree, red means I disagree. They convince event planners to purchase these trinkets for everyone in the audience because they think the audience is engaging when they're raising their hands to "vote." How can I say it nicely? This is the kind of tactic that gives *engagement* a bad rap. Forgive me if you're a speaker who's run the placard swindle (we've all done things we're not proud of), but that's not real engagement.

> The paradoxical truth is that audiences hate going to a keynote presentation only to be told to turn and talk to their neighbor—yet they love to *connect* with that neighbor.

The paradoxical truth is that audiences hate going to a keynote presentation only to be told to turn and talk to their neighbor—yet they love to *connect* with that neighbor. I'm not worried about connecting with an audience; I can usually do that, though some crowds are tougher than others. The trick we were looking for was what would connect a corporate audience with one another in a meaningful, memorable way.

Blue Glow Bad, Blue Glow Good

Math Fact: The likelihood that people in a corporate audience are going to take out their phones during the keynote speaker's presentation is 100 percent. Fair enough. Connectivity is their life force. They measure time in Excel columns. They are not eager for you or your little tricks.

We—and I am speaking for all speakers here—see it when you take out your phone. When you're a young speaker, this feels bad.

But the blue glow that emanates from a darkened ballroom is actually the most misunderstood of all blue glows. It's confusing for those just starting out—off-putting for obvious reasons but also mystifying—because sometimes the glow shines bluest when the presentation is really going well.

I've been in the game since phones were attached to buildings, but I, too, have bathed in the blue glow. Sometimes, an audience takes out their phones *because they are engaged.*

That sounds counterintuitive. Believe me, I know it can look really bad when an audience member pulls out the Google machine. But there comes a point in a successful keynote when the blue glow tells me I've got somebody hooked, because I know what they're doing with that thing: They're Googling to find out more about me.

"Psst, Margaret. Look . . . I didn't realize he was the Mentos guy."

"He was the guy on *Ellen* who destroyed her studio. He didn't even mention that."

"Did you know he did *SICK Science*? That stupid glockenspiel . . . "

Some friendly advice from an old-timer: If everything you have to share is in your forty-five minutes on stage, you're either a Zen master or you need to get busy working on more content to share with your audience. Admittedly, this is when it helps to have a career behind you, but there's no excuse for leaving seekers empty-handed.

In this day and age, if someone connects with you enough that they take it upon themselves to learn more about you, pat yourself on the back. This goes quadruple for corporate audiences. Time is money, and they really like money; if they want to invest even a few dollar-producing seconds to look you up, make it worth their while. If you've got more waiting for them, you've reached a level of engagement some people never do.

Good for the Goose,
Good for the Gander

We struggled with bringing a corporate event to life until we threw up our hands and said that folks are folks and connection is connection. We brought the Energy Sticks to a corporate event for a company called Workday. No one was there to make lesson plans, but what harm would it do to try our favorite old chestnut?

The differences between the Energy Stick routine and the voting placard may seem subtle, but those differences are everything:

- We hide the sticks (we only hide one per table) so that the audience has to find them. We're playing immediately.
- I fool them into discovering that the sticks work no matter how many people link up. "It only works with two! Don't try it with three!" (Teaching executives doesn't have to be so different from teaching third graders.)
- The experience *is* the message.

At the end of the demonstration, I tell everyone holding their table's Energy Stick to pass it to the person to their left.

"That person gets to take it home!"

Universal groans, punctuated by one cheer per table.

"Actually, you know what?" I say. "The nice folks at Workday bought you all an Energy Stick. They're down at the Workday booth. I'll see you there after the program."

Usually, I don't hang out at the booths, but Workday wanted me to, and the audience was so excited I told Carly we should hand out a few Energy Sticks. Carly recalls:

> We stood there for three hours. The line at the Workday booth was embarrassing. Everyone else in the exhibit hall was glaring. But everyone wanted to talk to Steve. They wanted

to share a story. This was a corporate audience, not teachers, and they all wanted to share a story about transformational engagement, because they had now made it their own.

I'd never signed an Energy Stick before. That day, I probably signed a thousand.

For all the time I've invested in learning how to stimulate engagement, it still takes my breath away when it shows up in an unexpected place and time. I've been saving the next story—the last story—because it's the best example I know of the almost mystical quality of highest engagement. It means everything to me, and I hope you will carry it with you as you try to make the world a better place—one community, one classroom, one student at a time.

The Lesson

- Engagement is not industry-specific. It's human-specific. It belongs in boardrooms, offices, classrooms, and leadership retreats.
- Fun, creativity, and connection aren't distractions from productivity; they're drivers of it.
- When you make space for curiosity and connection in corporate settings, you unlock new levels of collaboration and performance.
- The same principles that work with students work with executives: surprise, storytelling, relevance, and trust.

CHAPTER 35

MRS. LEIKAM

WHEN I FIRST HOPPED ON THE A/V CART AT WILLOW CREEK Elementary School, there was a first-grade teacher named JoAnn Leikam who was afraid of science experiments. She had done this thing with the kids years before where she siphoned a fish tank. They were going to clean the tank. She brought the bucket in, put the hose down inside the tank, and then said, "All you have to do is pull some of the air out, then it's going to drain on its own."

She started to pull up some of the air, and it came up a little too fast, and the fish water went into her mouth. She dropped the hose onto the floor and, as promised, it kept draining the tank, just not into the bucket. Mrs. Leikam was gagging, and the kids were screaming, "The fish! The fish!"

That was Mrs. Leikam's experience with hands-on science. It was her twenty-ninth year teaching when I started. I don't know how long it had been since she had conducted a science experiment.

"Steve Spangler can do whatever he wants with my class," she said. "Just count me out."

I loved her.

Year thirty is the big one for teachers, or it was then. The retirement year. They threw a retirement party for Mrs. Leikam a few weeks prior to the last day of school, but I didn't know about it. There was no email back then. I'm sure they had a little invitation they put in our mailboxes, but I was on the cart. I found out about it when I got to school on the last day.

At the end of the day, we were all outside waving goodbye to the kids on the buses, the year was over, and it hit me: Oh my gosh. Mrs. Leikam is retiring. I didn't bring a gift. I didn't do anything. What a schmuck. I thought I'd go to her room and leave a little note on her desk, at least.

There was a long pane of glass on all classroom doors there at the time, so you could always peek into a class and see what was going on. Mrs. Leikam was alone in her room, looking out the window. I thought, *You know what? I'm going to kick the door open one more time.*

BAM, I popped the door open and said, "Mrs. Leikam, you are out of here! You don't have to do this anymore! You're retired! You're gone!"

I was so emotionally illiterate I didn't realize I needed to read the room. She turned around and tears were flowing down her face.

"I'm so sorry," I said. "What happened?"

"Oh, Steve," she said in her distinctive Minnesota accent. "For twenty-nine years, I've known what to do on the last day of school. I put all the stuff in these boxes. I stack them into this mountain over here. They come in the summer to clean the classroom, and then next year, I come and take the boxes down and bring everything back out again. It just hit me a few minutes ago. Nobody ever tells you what to do on the *last* last day of school."

Nobody ever tells you what to do on the *last* last day of school.

"Mrs. Leikam, I wish I could tell you what to do," I said as I sheepishly headed toward the door. "I'm sorry . . ."

"Hang on, Steve." She went over to her mountain of boxes. She knew exactly which box to pull. "I know how much you love to teach science. So did I for many years. These are a few of the things that helped me teach science. Maybe they could help you. Would you like them?"

"Absolutely," I said. "Thank you." I took the box but didn't open it in front of her.

We hugged and I left. I found my A/V cart wherever I had stashed it. I couldn't wait to see what was in the box. A cool microscope? Classroom set of thermometers? As I pried open the cardboard flaps, the first thing I saw was a beaker with crusty coating on the inside next to a half-used box of Ziploc bags. There were file folders filled with worksheets and activity guides. I uncovered handouts from conferences she had attended that I never knew to ask her about. I found science experiment books signed by their authors. There were painted Styrofoam balls with string on them. That's it.

Then it hit me. The stuff in the box wasn't the gift. The gift was that she had given me the box in the first place. Although our friendship was only two years old, the experiences we shared during my periodic visits to her classroom connected us in a way that's hard to explain. This was her way of honoring me as a young teacher who shared her passion for inspiring children to become lifelong learners. For her, the box was overflowing with memories that spanned a thirty-year career.

She was giving of herself, because that's what teachers do.

Every year, Dr. Tarleton would bring retired teachers back to Willow Creek for a special luncheon. It was a brilliant principal move—probably a top-five all-time principal move.

I initially thought it was the stupidest thing ever, because all these old teachers were just going to tell us about golf or mah-jongg or something. I was twenty-nine years away from my first game of mah-jongg.

But two years after she gave me the box, JoAnn Leikam showed up for the retirement luncheon. Silver hair, wire-rim glasses, apple sweater. Fully retired teacher. I ran over and gave her a hug.

"Mrs. Leikam, I haven't seen you in forever."

"Steve," she said. "My name is JoAnn. You can call me JoAnn."

"Mrs. Leikam, I'm so happy to see you."

Dr. Tarleton would have all the retirees get up and tell us what was going on with them. JoAnn stood up first.

"It's kind of funny," she said. "I thought I retired two years ago and that was the end of the story. But it's not the end of the story. When you retire, the next chapter starts.

"I was sitting in Denny's with my husband one Sunday after church. A guy comes up to the table, and I thought he was warming up my coffee, so I kept talking to my husband. But the guy just stands there. I look up at him and realize he's not a server; he's just a guy. And he says, 'Excuse me, are you Mrs. Leikam?' I said, 'I'm JoAnn Leikam.' And he says, 'Do you remember me?' At that moment, I realized a student had come back.

"If you're lucky in your career, and things have really gone well, maybe they'll come back. The mere fact that he had graced me like this, that he gave me the gift of coming back and connecting with me, was marvelous. I had no idea who he was.

"But even if you don't know their name anymore, what they want more than anything else is to be remembered by you, so I said, 'Oh,

I do. I remember you, but you've just got to help me with the name.'
And he says, 'You called me Danny.' I probably had fifty Dannys over
my career. Thank God, he said his last name too. Then I remembered
him. Not a star student or a raving menace or anything, just a normal,
sweet kid. He said, 'Would you mind if I introduce you to my family?
Would that be OK?'

"I watched him walk away, and a little angel on my shoulder whispered into my ear, 'He's back. He came back after all this time.' He
brings his two kids over and his wife, and the wife is in the background going, 'Sorry, I'm sorry,' totally embarrassed that her husband
is disturbing our breakfast.

"'This is my first-grade teacher,' Danny said. 'This is my family.'

"I thought to myself, *This must've been pretty early on in my career
for him to be this old.*

"Danny said, 'I've got to ask you a question: Are you still doing the
solar system activity?'

"My mind was a blank. What was the solar system activity? I said,
'Honey, I've been retired. Help me again with that.'

"He says, 'You transformed the room into the solar system. There
were these planets that you had made, and we came in and we were
in a spaceship, and we went from planet to planet, and you told us
about the solar system.'

"I remembered. It must have been my second or third year of
teaching. Danny's idea of a transformed classroom was simply painted
Styrofoam balls hung from the ceiling with string to represent the
planets. In lieu of a great lesson plan, I flashed the lights on and off
and said, 'All aboard the spaceship to explore the solar system. Next
stop . . . Jupiter!' and the kids would run over to the largest of the
painted Styrofoam balls. It was nothing.

"Danny says, 'You know what I do for a living? I work for Lockheed Martin here in Littleton. I'm an engineer. I helped craft the solar panels that went on the Mars rover.'

"I didn't know what to say, so I didn't say anything.

"Danny says, 'That experience, the experience *you* created, changed my life absolutely forever. I had no idea that today would be the day where I got to say thanks.'"

Everyone at the luncheon was weeping openly, including me. I thought about the dusty Styrofoam balls on string that were still sitting in a box at my house.

"What am I trying to tell you?" said Mrs. Leikam. "Which days matter? Which activities count the most? You'll never know. You'll never know when you're going to connect with a kid, because when you connect with a kid and everything is perfect, the experience is life-changing. Every day matters.

"Could I ever say that I changed someone's life? Never. Because I didn't change anyone's life. All I did was create this opportunity for him to be able to find his passion, for him to be able to find his spark."

✳

I was telling Mrs. Leikam's story long before I ever came up with the idea of *best day ever*. But it hit me on stage one time during a keynote, and I became an emotional mess. I looked at Carly in the wings. *What the heck just happened?* It was a speech to two hundred teachers in Colorado, and it hit me like a ton of bricks: That's the secret. Mrs. Leikam had no clue what was so beautiful about the authentic experience she had created. She wasn't trying to do anything crazy. She wasn't trying to create the *Ellen Show*. She was just doing this solar system thing, and it connected.

Sometimes, even when we don't think we connect, we do ... and at the deepest level.

Sometimes, even when we don't think we connect, we do . . . and at the deepest level. As a leader, try to recognize the power you have in building experiences. It's incredible. It's a drug.

I don't often tell the JoAnn Leikam story in keynotes anymore. I love the story, but over time, I put it on my go-to speaker-story bookshelf, where it sat undisturbed for years. Then, two years ago, I did a teacher in-service in Florence. (This time it was Florence, Colorado. Still no cobblestones.) For some reason, when I woke up that morning in that hotel and looked out the window, I thought of the solar system story.

You know what? I thought. *I haven't done that in years.*

So, I shared the story as part of my wrap-up. I was a little out of practice, but all the elements came together, and judging from the tissues I saw scattered throughout the audience, the story of Mrs. Leikam and her journey throughout the solar system connected. When I got in the car to leave, I looked down at my phone and saw that Dr. Tarleton had left me a message. It's not uncommon for her to call. We've made it a point to keep in touch after all these years.

"Hey, Steve. It's Deena. I just wanted to reach out to let you know that JoAnn Leikam passed away yesterday. She died peacefully, in her sleep. I know she meant a lot to you, and I wanted to let you know."

Thanks, Mrs. Leikam.

The Lesson

- A simple act—done with care and intention—can echo for decades. You may never know which moment mattered most.
- The right teacher at the right time can change everything—sometimes with just a single word of encouragement.
- Impact isn't always immediate. Seeds planted by a teacher can bloom years later in unexpected ways.
- Influence isn't always immediate. Impact often reveals itself in the rearview mirror, years later. We all have the power to be someone's "Mrs. Leikam"—someone who sees potential and calls it out.
- Teaching and leadership are legacy work. Even the smallest moments can echo for a lifetime.

THE ECHO OF ENGAGEMENT

F YOU'VE MADE IT THIS FAR, SOMETHING IN THESE PAGES STRUCK A chord. Maybe you've been reflecting on your own experiences—times when you created a connection, when you felt the energy shift as engagement took hold, or maybe moments when you completely missed the mark and didn't know why. Maybe you're questioning whether you've been too focused on the mechanics of leadership and not enough on the experience itself. Or maybe you just enjoy stories of flaming wallets, flying potatoes, and near disasters turned into learning moments.

Whatever brought you here, I hope one thing is clear: Engagement isn't a formula. It's an invitation.

Likewise, leadership isn't about commanding. It's about *creating*—designing moments that invite people in through the interplay of experience, connection, and engagement. We've looked at why people lean in, why they check out, and how engagement—when it's legit—is built on trust, curiosity, and shared experience.

Now, as we close, I'd like to offer one final piece to help all this stick.

The Leadership Paradox:
It's Not About You

One of the hardest truths about engagement is this: The moment you make it about yourself, you lose. The flaming wallet routine didn't work in Florence, Alabama, because I was performing *at* people, not *with* them. My audience hadn't been invited into the moment; I was *showing them something* instead of *sharing something with them*. And when engagement is self-serving, people sense it instantly.

Every successful engagement story in this book—whether in a classroom, on a stage, or in a corporate boardroom—was built from an experience crafted for others. Real engagement happens when people see *themselves* in the moment, when they aren't just observers, but participants. That's why magic, science demonstrations, and even well-timed jokes have the power to draw people in. They surrender *ownership*. True leaders don't steal the spotlight. They hand out the matches and let others light the fire.

True leaders don't steal the spotlight. They hand out the matches and let others light the fire.

Engagement might not manifest itself in front of you. That's OK. Little Danny's *best day ever* changed his life because his first-grade teacher created an experience that allowed him to connect. That may have been the only year Mrs. Leikam ever did the Styrofoam solar system activity, but now we have a rover on Mars.

The *Best Day Ever* Mindset

Engagement is a habit. It's a mindset. It's a way of moving through the world that seeks to bring other people along for the ride and then lets them drive.

When you start seeing the world through the lens of engagement, you stop asking, *How do I make them listen?* and you start asking, *How do I create something they want to be part of?*

That shift is everything.

A truly great leader, teacher, or performer is someone who leaves people feeling more capable, more connected, and more alive than they were before. They aren't the hero of the story—they hand the cape to someone else.

Every day is not the "best day ever." The reason that mantra has stuck with me is because the *best day ever* mindset forces me to look for engagement everywhere. It reminds me that every interaction is an opportunity. Every moment—whether in front of ten thousand people or one child watching a science experiment—is a chance to create something meaningful.

The Ripple Effect

My dad's real magic was making nerdy, shy, quiet kids blossom. He could make them talk. He could make them happy. They came to every magic class, even if they didn't want to do the tricks. It didn't matter. They just loved being there. The experience encouraged them to connect. Who knows what kind of engagement that led to.

A famous statement attributed to Maya Angelou always comes to mind when I think about those classes: "People will forget what you said. People will forget what you did. But people will never forget how you made them feel." The magic of engagement is in what happens next.

The real power of the fire wallet or the exploding soda bottle is in the kid who goes home and can't stop talking about it. It's in the teacher who walks back into their classroom with a renewed sense of purpose. It's in the corporate leader who stops focusing on productivity hacks and starts thinking about creating an environment where people want to show up.

Engagement echoes. It carries. And when it's built on genuine connection, it lasts far longer than the moment itself.

As you close this book and start thinking about what you'll do next, I hope you'll focus on these guiding principles. Start thinking like an experience designer. Look for the cues that tell you when people are leaning in, when curiosity sparks, and when connection begins. Pay attention to those moments, because they hold the key to everything.

And when in doubt, remember this: Leaders create shared experiences. Those experiences open the door to real connection. And real connection is where engagement takes root.

That's the whole game. And now, it's your turn to play.

ACKNOWLEDGMENTS

*T*HE *ENGAGEMENT EFFECT* IS THE RESULT OF A LIFETIME SPENT IN THE company of family, friends, business partners, and generous mentors who guided, challenged, and believed in me through every wild idea and ambitious goal.

To my wife, Renée—my North Star. This book simply wouldn't exist without your wisdom, insight, support, kindness, and (yes) financial savvy. Your ability to see the long game, especially when I'm wrapped up in the moment, has made all the difference. When I needed a push, you gave it with love and just the right words: *"This book isn't going to write itself. Get back to your desk and write."* That's true love. You didn't just believe in the work—you believed in the *why*. Your presence is woven into every chapter, and the stories in these pages are a love letter to that legacy.

To my three sons, Jack, Mark, and Scott—thank you for every backyard experiment and kitchen chemistry mishap you embraced with wide eyes and willing hands. You challenge me to think differently and to live a life filled with wonder, curiosity, and discovery. I'll always cherish our dinner conversations—filled with laughter, questions, and memories that matter.

To Carly Reed—thank you for over two decades of loyalty, brilliance, and friendship. You are the architect of so many experiences that bring people together. Your fingerprints are all over this book and every meaningful endeavor I've taken on in the last twenty years.

Special thanks to:

- **Zack Gresham**, for watching hours of video tapes and digging through stories to help uncover the lessons worth sharing. Your insight, care, and patience gave shape to a wild mess of stories and science experiments and turned them into a book worth reading.
- **Allen Harris, Billie Brownell, Phil Newman, Jennifer Gingerich, and the rest of the team at Forefront Books and Mark Spangler**—your editorial skills shaped this manuscript in more ways than you know.
- **George Stevens**, for bringing your design genius to the cover and giving this story a visual identity that matches its message.
- Fellow authors and speakers **Skip Prichard, Scott McKain, Eric Chester, Theo Androus, and Deb Fine**—thank you for your guidance, wisdom, and willingness to share the hard-earned lessons from inside the publishing world.
- **Dr. Nido Qubein**—thank you for the extraordinary opportunity to be part of the High Point University family. Your bold vision for what's possible in education is nothing short of inspiring. I'm honored to work alongside your world-class faculty and passionate students as we reimagine how STEM experiences can spark curiosity, creativity, and connection at the highest level.
- **My mother-in-law and father-in-law, Mae and Lou Lamberson**—thank you for trusting me enough to let your daughter climb into a magic box so I could slice her into three pieces and put her back together again. That's real love—and a good sense of humor. I'm especially grateful that you both changed careers midstream to help Renée and me build Steve Spangler Science and Be Amazing Toys from the ground up.

The products you crafted with your own hands found their way into classrooms around the world, helping thousands of teachers create unforgettable learning experiences. There's no way to measure the lives you impacted—but it's more than you'll ever know.

- **Mark and Sue Scharenbroich**—you continue to be our gold standard in business and in life. Your influence reaches far beyond these pages, and Renée and I are on this journey because of you.

- **To my mom and dad, Kitty and Bruce Spangler**—thank you for the gift of the most wonderfully unconventional childhood a kid could ever ask for. Growing up in a family of professional magicians didn't just give me great stories (and there are plenty of those)—it gave me a lens through which to see the world. Your influence isn't just part of my backstory—it's foundational to the engagement philosophy that drives this entire book. You taught me that real magic happens in the space between people, in the shared moment where curiosity meets wonder. The fire-eating, the color-changing liquids, the thousands of silk handkerchiefs, and the magic props—all of it was unforgettable. But what stayed with me most was the idea that every moment is a chance to create connection.

- **And to the thousands of students, teachers, and parents I've had the privilege to learn alongside**—thank you for saying yes to the mess, the noise, the flaming books, and the flying potatoes. You helped me discover what engagement really looks like.

The Engagement Effect may have my name on the cover, but every chapter reflects the fingerprints of the people who have helped me understand what it means to truly connect, lead, and engage. Thank you for helping me find the magic…and now to share it with you.

ENDNOTES

1 Shuck & Wollard, 2010; Shuck and Rose, 2013.

2 Catherine Bailey, Adrian Madden, Kerstin Alfes, et al., "Evaluating the Evidence on Employee Engagement and Its Potential Benefits to NHS Staff: A Narrative Synthesis of the Literature," *Health Services and Delivery Research*, No. 3.26, NIHR Journals Library.

3 Catherine Bailey., et al, "Evaluating the Evidence of Employee Engagement."; William A. Kahn, "Psychological Conditions of Personal Engagement and Disengagement at Work," *Academy of Management Journal* 33, no. 4 (December 1990): 692-724, https://www.jstor.org/stable/256287.

4 Catherine Bailey., et al, "Evaluating the Evidence of Employee Engagement."; M. S. Christian, A. S. Garza, and J. E. Slaughter, "Work Engagement: A Quantitative Review and Test of Its Relations with Task and Contextual Performance," *Personnel Psychology* 64, no. 1 (2011): 89-136, https://psycnet.apa.org/record/2011-03454-004.

5 Lauren A. Keating and Peter A. Heslin, "The Potential Role of Mindsets in Unleashing Employee Engagement," *Human Resource Management Review* 25, no. 4 (December 2015): 329-41, https://www.sciencedirect.com/science/article/abs/pii/S1053482215000091.

6 A. B. Bakker, "The Social Psychology of Work Engagement: State of the Field," *Career Development International* 27, no. 1 (2022): 36-53, https://psycnet.apa.org/record/2022-54603-002.

7 M. H. Jin and B. McDonald, "Understanding Employee Engagement in the Public Sector: The Role of Immediate Supervisor, Perceived Organizational Support, and Learning Opportunities," *American Review of Public Administration* 47, no. 8 (2017): 881-97, https://psycnet.apa.org/record/2017-47023-002.

8 A. B. Bakker, E. Demerouti, and A. Sanz-Vergel, "Job Demands—Resources Theory: Ten Years Later," *Annual Review of Organizational Psychology and Organizational Behavior* 10 (2023): 25-53, https://psycnet.apa.org/record/2023-48430-002.

9 A. J. Martin and M. Dowson, "Interpersonal Relationships, Motivation,

Engagement, and Achievement: Yields for Theory, Current Issues, and Educational Practice," *Review of Educational Research* 79, no. 1 (2009): 327-65, https://psycnet. apa.org/record/2010-06906-010.

10 William A. Kahn, "To Be Fully There: Psychological Presence at Work," *Human Relations* 45, no. 4 (1992): https://journals.sagepub.com/doi/ abs/10.1177/001872679204500402.

11 T. Sitzmann and J. M. Weinhardt, "Training Engagement Theory: A Multilevel Perspective on the Effectiveness of Work-related Training," *Journal of Management* 44, no. 2 (2018): 732-56, https://psycnet.apa.org/record/2015-11137-001.

12 Ellen Beattie, "The Power of Positive Leadership: An Examination of Leadership Strategies Based on Positive Psychology, Applied Neuroscience, and the Learning Sciences," *Resource for Adult Education* 8, no. 2 (Fall 2019): 52-63, https://eric. ed.gov/?id=EJ1253163.

13 Paul J. Zak, "The Neuroscience of Trust: Management Behaviors that Foster Employee Engagement," *Harvard Business Review*, January–February 2017.

14 Aditya Malik, "The Science of Employee Engagement: Optimizing Well-Being with Neuroscience and Biometrics," *Forbes*, November 19, 2024.

15 Doo Hun Lim et al., "Neuroscientism: the Neuroscience of Learning," *European Journal of Training and Development* 43, no. 7-8 (2019): 619-42, https://eric. ed.gov/?id=EJ1227740.; Richard P. Keeling and Richard H. Hersh, *We're Losing Our Minds: Rethinking American Higher Education*, "The Neuroscience of Learning" (Palgrave Macmillan, 2011).

16 Interview with Dr. Amy Holcombe and Dr. Dearing Blankmann, January 17, 2025.

17 "5 Steps to Building an 'Extraordinary' Successful Business and Life," *MSP Success*, September 30, 2021, https://mspsuccess.com/2021/09/5-steps-to-building-an-ex-traordinarily-successful-business-and-life/.

18 Dale Carnegie, *How to Win Friends and Influence People* (Simon & Schuster, 2009).

19 As you read this account, please keep in mind that this was 1992. School was different then. You could get away with the element of surprise, even the occasional explosion, without sending the building into lockdown. Hats off to every teacher and student in today's troubled world, and to everyone working to fix what's broken.

20 Jeremy Moser, "12 TikTok Metrics You Should Track to Measure Content Performance and Improve Engagement," *Planable* (blog), January 13, 2025.

ABOUT THE AUTHOR

STEVE SPANGLER HAS SPENT HIS CAREER PROVING THAT THE MOST powerful engagement begins with experience. A bestselling author, two-time Emmy Award winner, and host of the nationally syndicated television series *DIY Sci*, Steve is best known for turning ordinary moments into unforgettable learning experiences.

Steve first gained international attention as the creator of YouTube's original viral science video—teaching millions how to launch a Diet Coke geyser with Mentos. That one explosive moment helped redefine how science is shared, taught, and celebrated online. Today, his science videos have generated more than 4.5 billion views across YouTube, TikTok, Instagram, and Facebook, igniting curiosity in classrooms, homes, and boardrooms around the globe.

For more than twenty-five years, Steve's books, live events, and hands-on experiments have helped educators and parents turn passive learners into active participants. As the STEM Educator-in-Residence at High Point University and a member of the prestigious Speaker Hall of Fame, he works with educators, business leaders, and organizations to create transformational experiences that spark curiosity, build trust, and drive engagement that lasts.

With more than 2,100 television appearances and a global reputation for making science accessible and unforgettable, Steve's work empowers leaders at every level to turn everyday interactions into extraordinary opportunities for engagement, innovation, and impact.

If you ever saw the chaos he brought to *The Ellen DeGeneres Show*—flaming soap bubbles, smoke rings, flying potatoes—you'll understand why Ellen called him "the science teacher you always wanted in school…because the fire department shows up twice a year."

To inquire about media appearances or booking opportunities, visit SteveSpangler.com.